To Megan, Adam and Rupert

First published 1976 by Methuen & Co Ltd
11 New Fetter Lane, London EC4P 4EE
© 1976 Nick Heather
Printed in Great Britain by
Richard Clay (The Chaucer Press), Ltd
Bungay, Suffolk

ISBN (hardback) 0 416 81850 1
ISBN (paperback) 0 416 81860 9

We are grateful to Grant McIntyre of Open Books Publishing Ltd
for assistance in the preparation of this series

Contents

Editor's Introduction

I will be very sorry if this powerful book by Nick Heather is considered just a slot-filler, the standard concession to the trendy lefties. Nick raises fundamental questions about academic and applied psychology which we all have to consider. As he clearly demonstrates, the notion of value-free objective science and technology is untenable. Nick Heather has one view of the nature of the values and assumptions underlying psychology; David Legge, in his equally lucid volume (A1), has quite another. Read the two together!

Radical Perspectives in Psychology belongs to Unit F of *Essential Psychology*. What unifies the books in this unit is the concept of change, not only in people but also in psychology. Both the theory and the practice of the subject are changing fast. The assumptions underlying the different theoretical frameworks are being revealed and questioned. New basic assumptions are being advocated, and consequently new frameworks constructed. One example is the theoretical framework of 'mental illness': the assumptions of normality and abnormality are being questioned, together with the notions of 'the cause', 'the cure', and 'the doctor-patient relationship'. As a result, different frameworks are developing, and different professional practices gradually being initiated. There are, though, various social and political structures which tend to inhibit the translation of changing theory into changing practice.

7

One interesting change is the current aversion to theoretical frameworks which liken human beings to something else. For example, among many psychologists the analogy of the human being as a computer which characterizes Unit A is in less favour than the concepts of development (Unit C) and the person (Unit D).

Essential Psychology as a whole is designed to reflect this changing structure and function of psychology. The authors are both academics and professionals, and their aim has been to introduce the most important concepts in their areas to beginning students. They have tried to do so clearly but have not attempted to conceal the fact that concepts that now appear central to their work may soon be peripheral. In other words, they have presented psychology as a developing set of views of man not as a body of received truth. Readers are not intended to study the whole series in order to 'master the basics'. Rather, since different people may wish to use different theoretical fromeworks for their own purposes, the series has been designed so that each title stands on its own. But it is possible that if the reader has read no psychology before, he will enjoy individual books more if he has read the introductions (A1, B1, etc.) to the units to which they belong. Readers of the units concerned with applications of psychology (E, F) may benefit from reading all the introductions.

A word about references in the text to the work of other writers – e.g. 'Smith (1974)'. These occur where the author feels he must acknowledge an important concept or some crucial evidence by name. The book or article referred to will be listed in the References (which double as Name Index) at the back of the book. The reader is invited to consult these sources if he wishes to explore topics further. A list of general Further Reading is also to be found at the back of this book.

We hope you enjoy psychology.

Peter Herriot

I

Introduction

First things first. The word radical is defined as 'of the root' (OED). It does *not* mean 'hot-headed', 'extremist', 'irresponsible', 'describing the views of an unimportant minority' or 'not worthy of serious consideration'. These are all connotations of the word which are encouraged by those who find radical views threatening. If the criticisms of psychology and psychiatry presented in this book are radical, it is because they challenge the assumptions of those disciplines *at the root*. And if changes in psychology and psychiatry are urged as part of a larger, radical change in society, it is because that society needs to be transformed *at the root*.

The title I originally wanted for this book was simply 'Radical Psychology', but this would have caused confusion with the recently published book of the same name by Phil Brown (1973). So, we decided on the present title. However, although it is true that there are various, independent objections to such a large field of human endeavour as psychology, I continue to have doubts about the word 'perspectives'. This is because there *is* a radical movement in psychology. This movement includes people of differing political persuasions – some Marxists, some libertarians, some both, and some who cannot affix a label to themselves but who incriminate psychology and psychiatry in the misery, injustice, and oppression they see all around them. But most of these people would agree, I hope, with most of what is written in this book. I have therefore taken it as my task to describe this radical consensus as straightforwardly and comprehensively as is possible in the limited space available.

In the next chapter will be found a critique of modern academic psychology. To call this collection of irrelevance, triviality and downright silliness a science is preposterous. Psychology has the appearance of a science, the trappings and jargon of a science, but it *is* not a science. It is a species of profound self-deception. Chapter 3 attempts to reveal the basis of this self-deception and presents the main thesis of the book – that, for the most part, current psychology is not the objective and value-free enterprise it is usually taken for, but is instead a modern form of ideology.

Chapter 4 portrays the most practical illustration of this ideological content, in psychiatry. I have devoted a disproportionate amount of space to this topic because of the prominence it has acquired in radical thinking. The remaining chapters complete our understanding of the practical implications of ideological psychology, describing briefly the applied areas of the discipline and by specific examples of oppression in which psychology and psychiatry have played an important part.

Incidentally, my friends in the Women's Movement, if any, may like to note that I have consistently referred to the reader as female and have tended to use the third person, 'she', while reserving the generic 'man' for the human race. I have done this because I cannot be bothered with brackets, as in (s)he and (wo)man, but could not see why convention should not for once be inverted.

2
Positivism and psychology

The radical movement in psychology has directed its criticism at two main targets – 'behavourism' and 'psychiatry'. These are both very rude words in the radical vocabulary.

At first sight these targets do not appear to have very much in common. As the reader will probably be aware, the theory and practice of psychiatry was developed independently of academic psychology. Psychiatry is part of medical science, employs medical concepts and modes of thought and is practised by the medically qualified. Academic psychology, on the other hand, has not considered the problems of 'mental illness' to be a legitimate area of scientific inquiry, chiefly because these problems were not amenable to study in the laboratory. It is true that in the last decade or so there has been a rapid expansion in the field of clinical psychology, in which theories developed by psychologists have been applied practically in mental hospitals, but this expansion has had little impact on the main body of psychiatric thought as yet. The point here is that if the radical critique is to be coherent, we need a larger concept which will embrace and unify the objectionable aspects of both behaviourism and psychiatry.

There are other reasons why this larger concept is necessary. The term 'behaviourism' itself is unsatisfactory if it is intended to refer to all the characteristics of modern, academic psychology that radicals dislike. There are many psychologists whose work is the object of radical scorn who would deny that they were behaviourists in any meaningful sense. They may be concerned to account for perceptual or cognitive processes which are certainly not capable of being directly and publicly observed, in the sense that J. B. Watson, the founder of behaviourism, required that all variables used in psychology should be. Again, if they adopt a cybernetic approach, they will describe man as a self-regulating machine, which appears a far cry from the 'push and pull' model of stimulus-response behaviourism. In actual practice radicals tend to use the term 'behaviourism' loosely, but with some justification, to describe the mechanistic kind of psychology they were taught, or are being taught, in their courses. But it is a poor tactic to give your opponent a label he does not acknowledge.

A similar need for a larger concept exists in psychiatry. There are two dominant schools of psychiatric thought – organic psychiatry and psychoanalysis. In organic psychiatry, mental illness is viewed as the result of biochemical disturbances and it is this that ultimately justifies the use of drugs and electroconvulsive therapy (ECT) towards which most radical protest has been directed. The psychoanalytic school, based on the theories of Freud and his followers, sees mental illness quite differently, as the consequence of psychological conflicts with no reference to bodily malfunctions. The treatment implied here is, of course, psychoanalysis or some derivative form of psychotherapy. While some radicals would accept psychoanalysis, most wish to say 'a plague on both your houses'. Once more we need a superordinate concept with which to castigate both kinds of psychiatric viewpoint.

Let me now end the suspense by stating that the concept we need is that of *positivism*. Let me also anticipate a fuller discussion by stating the main property of positivism as revealed in all the various brands of psychology radicals object to. It is that they all, in their different ways, *use science to dehumanize man*.

What is positivism?

Strictly speaking, positivism is a position in epistemology, that branch of philosophy devoted to the theory of knowledge. As such, it is concerned to provide answers to questions like what is it possible to know, how may we be certain that we know something, what is a meaningful problem capable of solution and what is not, and what rules should we use to decide upon these matters. In this sense positivism is also a school of thought in the philosophy of science.

More generally speaking, the term positivism is used to refer to a broadly defined movement in the history of man's intellectual development, the distinguishing feature of which is *the attempt to apply to the affairs of man the methods and principles of the natural sciences*. To understand more fully the nature of this movement it may be instructive to examine the origins of positivism at the beginning of the nineteenth century.

The term was coined by the French philosopher Auguste Comte, who is also often credited with being the founder of sociology. Comte was disturbed by the political disruption which followed the French Revolution and wished to see society organized in a more rational, ordered fashion. The means to achieve this end he saw in 'science', which in the two centuries preceding Comte's had achieved some remarkable and prestigious triumphs. Thus, Comte's principal contribution to philosophy was the suggestion that human behaviour, institutions, and political organization could be investigated and ultimately brought under control by the same kind of methods that, say, a chemist uses to investigate the interaction of chemical substances.

Now the reader may find nothing very startling in this suggestion of Comte's. She may have agreed at the outset of her studies that psychology should be a science and that it must therefore copy the methods of physics, chemistry, and biology, since this, she believes, is precisely what being a science means. If the reader does hold this view, it is because of the pervasive influence of positivism in our culture. The positivistic attitude has become something we have inherited from earlier generations and, like other aspects of inherited culture, it forms and constrains the way we think. It has become, like the family or private property, part of the 'natural order of things' which we tend to accept with unquestioning compliance. The value of adopting an historical perspective in any area of study is that it teaches us that what we previously regarded as inevitable was not always so and might therefore be changed.

With this in mind, we see that positivism is a relatively recent and, I hope, short-lived episode in the history of thought. Before Comte, in the Classical Age, the dominant view of man had been that of a rational creature whose behaviour, in contrast to that of lower forms of life, resulted from a privileged access to Reason. Indeed, his scientific achievements were the most compelling and triumphant illustration of this Reason, enabling him to master his physical environment and adjust it to his choice. Few had seriously envisaged the possibility that man should, as it were, turn this new mastery against himself. This was precisely Comte's idea in creating the new science of sociology, by means of which the future organization of society was to be controlled according to established laws by a scientific élite. Interestingly enough, Comte had no place in his scheme of things for a specific science of psychology. But his profound influence on the entire range of human sciences derives from his insistence on the *unity of the sciences*.

It would be a mistake to see Comte's work as marking a sharp division between the classical and positivistic views of man. In the seventeenth century Thomas Hobbes had advocated the application of the newly discovered Galilean laws of motion to the behaviour of man. On the other hand, the classical perspective continues, despite positivistic inroads, to dominate the practice of law. Nevertheless, it was in the nineteenth century that the influence of positivism on human science grew apace. As far as psychology is concerned, there are two significant dates marking the progress of positivism and illustrating also different aspects of its effect upon psychology, one theoretical and one methodological. In 1859 Darwin published *The Origin of Species*, making it possible for psychology to be placed squarely in the ranks of the biological sciences and leading to that view of psychology which sees man as 'organism'. In 1879 Wundt opened the first psychological laboratory at Leipzig, thus creating the precedent for the experimental basis on which academic psychology has subsequently rested. Later, these theoretical and methodological principles were united in the rat behaviourism which dominated the second quarter of the twentieth century.

Before leaving Comte we should note another aspect of his work which has considerable relevance to the radical critique. Towards the end of his life Comte's thought developed into an all-embracing vision of a future society, which some commentators have seen as the result of a mental derangement, while others consider it a logical extension of his earlier views. In particular, Comte proposed a secular religion, to be known as the Religion of Humanity, which was intended to replace existing forms of religious life. This new religion was to be structured after the model of the Catholic Church, with a positive pope, priesthood, and specially erected positive temples. The dogmas of the religion were, of course, the doctrines expounded by Comte and the laws of science. Although Comte intended this vision to be construed in a quite literal sense, it may serve as a kind of elaborate metaphor for what radicals believe is a very real feature of modern, industrial society. The idea is simply that science and scientists have replaced religion and priests as the dominant source of authority in our society. This authority is based on the faith on the part of non-scientists in the infallibility of scientific pronouncements, and the conviction that only science can provide a solution to man's problems. As was the case in the days of religious domination, ordinary people are led to renounce personal responsibility for the rules they live by and accept definitions of reality provided for them by the scientific expert. To be sure, scientific dogmas may be used by those with political power to further their own interests, in exactly the same way that Renaissance princes used the disguise of religion to further theirs. But wherever the ultimate power lies, the mystification of ordinary people is accomplished by means of the supreme moral authority of science. Thus science has become the new 'opium of the people'. The term *scientism* has been used to denote this quasi-religious function of science in society.

Logical positivism

The subsequent course of philosophical positivism was marked by a much more cautious and sober approach to epistemological problems. The culmination of the movement occurred in the 1920s with the formation of the Vienna Circle, a group of philosophers, mathematicians, and scientists who set out with apostolic zeal to reform philosophy and purge it of metaphysics. Although these thinkers eschewed the utopian aspects of Comte's work, there nevertheless remained a firm commitment to science as providing the only vehicle of human progress.

In another sense logical positivism was more extreme than earlier versions. For, whereas previously so-called metaphysical questions and questions of value and morality were regarded merely as unscientific, they were now legislated out of human discourse as being meaningless pseudo-problems. The only statements worthy of consideration were scientific statements whose contents were capable of being publicly verified, and discussion of anything else was simply a waste of breath. Unfortunately for the positivists, a satisfactory definition of verification and hence a usable distinction between meaningful and meaningless questions are problems they are still wrestling with. Nevertheless, it is the strict separation in principle between the world of science and the world of values, and the relegation of the latter to the realm of nonsense, which has had a disastrous effect upon our intellectual culture. This general effect is evidenced every time a scientist is heard dismissing the moral consequences of his research as meaningless. The author once had occasion to ask a psychologist engaged upon designing market research about the effect of his work upon society. Did he think that the development of new products should be determined by what it was possible, with the aid of market research, to sell, or should considerations of use and benefit to the consumer weigh more heavily? I was met with the reply that this was a 'metaphysical question'. This man was using the teachings of logical positivism, somewhat inaccurately, to justify his moral irresponsibility. I shall return to the issue of the ideological function of positivism in the next chapter.

In their attitude to psychology the logical positivists were, as might be expected, strong supporters of early behaviourism. In the behaviourists' rejection of introspection as a method and in their refusal to grant subjective experience any place whatever in scientific discourse, the positivists found a reflection of their own insistence that science be based on descriptions of elementary facts. These basic facts corresponded to 'atoms of experience' – simple, unequivocal perceptions about which, they contended, there could be no disagreement between observers. All statements used in science were required to be reducible to these simple units of observation and, indeed, the very meaning of a scientific statement was held to be identical with the method used to verify its constituent parts. This leads on to the notion of *operationalism*, much used in psychology, whereby the definition of any psychological variable is given by the 'operations' which are used to measure it. Thus, 'intelligence is what the test measures'; that is, the meaning of intelligence is no more and no less than a score on an intelligence test the psychologist has seen fit to devise.

A further consequence of logical positivism for psychology is contained in the concept of *physicalism*. Since all statements in a science must be reduced to simpler propositions describing the physical behaviour of bodies, it follows that all valid propositions must be capable of being translated into the language of physics. According to this view, psychology will be swallowed up in the universal science of physics when it has attained a sufficient degree of maturity. This is an extreme form of the general principle of *reductionism* which in psychology usually implies the belief that everything in human behaviour can ultimately be accounted for in the workings of the brain and nervous system.

A more general influence of logical positivism has to do with the nature of scientific inquiry itself. For the positivists a science is constituted by nothing more than a collection of facts. The role of theory in such a science is restricted to the organization of these facts into a logically coherent system from which the facts may be deduced and new facts predicted. In other words, there is no place in this conception of science for the operation of imagination. It is worth noting at this point that what the Vienna Circle set out to do was to prescribe how science *should* be done, not to describe how it *is* actually done. This introduces the question, what is the task of a philosophy of science. Is it to dictate to scientists how they should do their work, or is it, more modestly, to demonstrate the rules and methods by which successful science is accomplished? Harré and Secord (1972) have argued convincingly that real science, as opposed to science as prescribed by the positivists, cannot proceed without the controlled use of imagination. Moreover, this imagination is used to construct ideas of things and processes which are unobservable in order to explain what we do actually see. It will be noted how this account of how science really does proceed differs markedly from the positivists' notions of what it should be doing. In Harré's view, the influence of logical positivism on psychology has contributed largely to its narrow methodology and trivial content, whereas the adoption of a realist philosophy of science frees psychology from many of its self-imposed constraints and leads on to a radically different conception of psychology as science. I shall return to what kind of science this is later.

Positivistic psychology and its alternatives

Although it is clear that philosophical positivism has had some direct influence on established psychology, the question precisely what aspects of modern psychology were derived from which particular brand of positivism is one for the professional philosopher and lies outside my competence. More important for our present purposes is the understanding of most academic psychology as 'positivistic' in the larger sense, that it forms part of the attempt to force the study of man into the framework of the natural sciences, and it is in this sense that I want to use the word in the term 'positivistic psychology'.

I intend now to examine in more detail some of the consequences of this attempt to make psychology a science like physics and to present non-positivistic alternatives in each case. I have decided to divide the material into three somewhat arbitrary and overlapping sections of causes, facts, and methods. I shall postpone a discussion of psychiatry to a later chapter and confine my attention here to modern academic psychology.

Causes

Although psychology has come a long way from the early days of behaviourism, it is crucial to recognize that it is still fundamentally *mechanistic* in its account of man. By mechanistic I mean simply that man continues to be described as though he were some complicated piece of machinery. Thus, he is regarded as something passive and inert, propelled into motion only by the action of some force, either external or internal, upon him. His behaviour is fully explicable, in principle, in terms of 'causes' which he has no control over; if we could only know everything that had happened to him up to the present time we could predict his behaviour, whether he liked it or not, with absolute certainty. These are some of the implicit assumptions underlying the notion of causality that most psychologists have in their heads.

The reader will observe how this simplistic cause-and-effect model of human behaviour derives directly from how most of us think physics is done. More accurately, it derives from nineteenth century physics, for it is a supreme irony that modern physics has long abandoned the mechanistic determinism of the last century which psychologists, in their anxiety to be seen as respectable scientists, continue to copy. Be that as it may, it is a fair statement that the dominant conception of causation allowed by established psychology in this country is one ideally suited to describing the behaviour of billiard balls.

This reference to the billiard table is appropriate, for it was a device used extensively by the eighteenth century philosopher, David Hume, to explain his ideas. It is upon Hume's thought that the majority of psychologists base their understanding of causation, whether they know it or not. In fact, Hume denied that it was permissible to speak of 'causes', since this was again a metaphysical notion – a meaningless idea which refers to nothing in the real world. Modern psychology has, by and large, followed him in this and seeks merely to discover 'antecedent events', which precede some given piece of behaviour with sufficient regularity to enable the same behaviour to be predicted in a new situation. The task of psychology is seen as the collection of such observed regularities, which then become the basic data from which theories of behaviour are built, in the way recommended by the logical positivists. In early behaviourism, the antecedent events were presumed to be restricted to events in the outside world; they were the 'stimuli' which called forth 'responses' from the passive organism. Later, when such a crude model met with little explanatory success, even for the behaviour of rats, the place of organismic or 'intervening' variables came to be recognized. Now stimuli were no longer thought of as directly linked to responses but were mediated in their effect by factors internal to the organism. But, and this is the important point, whatever modifications were made to the basic model and however sophisticated the piece of machinery became that man was supposed to resemble, the *paradigm* remained unchanged. Human beings continued to be regarded by psychologists as some kind of helpless clockwork puppet, jerked into life only when something happened to it.

What is the alternative to this positivistic view of human behaviour? It is simply this – to credit human beings with the ability to be the causes of their own behaviour; to regard them, in other words, as *agents* (see A7). Let us note straight away that this alternative view of man is fully consistent with commonsense: that is, with our natural and immediate understanding of ourselves and others. In the everyday world, we naturally take ourselves to be responsible for what we are doing – to be able to choose between various alternatives open to us and act on these choices. Thus our commonsense understanding of what we do, when we are not being 'scientific' psychologists, assumes at the outset that we intend our actions and this assumption is embedded in the language we use to describe our own and others' behaviour. This is what we mean when we use the word 'person'; we refer to things that we know have the same ability as ourselves to intend their actions and to be aware that they are intending them. This is also how the word is meant when one proposes, as I am doing here, *a science of persons*.

Before proceeding further, it may be wise to justify the appeal to ordinary language which has been made above since the reader may already have been indoctrinated in the pernicious attitude which holds the language of the non-expert in patronizing contempt. Before it can proceed, any science must have a more or less worked out conceptual apparatus within which to place its observations and make them meaningful. In ordinary language we already have an elaborate and highly refined conceptual tool, developed over thousands of years of talking to each other. For as long as men have been alive they have been psychologists, trying to puzzle out why they and their friends do what they do, and developing along the way a set of distinctions referring to human behaviour far richer than any scientist could devise starting from scratch, even if she could ever be successful in ridding her new language of the influence of the old one. To be sure, the conceptual scheme of ordinary language is not without ambiguities and contradictions but it is precisely the task of *conceptual analysis*, as practised in modern philosophy, to analyse ordinary language and make it fit for scientific purposes. It is because psychologists are usually trained to adopt the purblind view that philosophy is irrelevant to their needs that the richness of ordinary language as the conceptual foundation of their science is lost to them. Only by a change in attitude to philosophy in general and the analysis of ordinary language in particular can psychology hope to avoid the force of Wittgenstein's (1953) famous charge that 'psychology has experimental methods and conceptual confusion'.

Returning to the distinction between actions and movements, it is interesting to note that primitive man, so we are reliably informed, made the mistake of describing inanimate objects as though they were men and women; for example, the sun was personified and given the ability to plan his course across the sky. I would claim that it is equally primitive to make the reverse mistake and describe men and women as though they were inanimate objects.

The usual objection to a science of persons which regards human beings as capable of intending their actions is to say that it is *voluntaristic*. This means that it credits us with free will, the ability to choose our actions. Although, as we shall see, a science of persons need not postulate a total freedom but only a freedom within limits, it is true that this science must opt for voluntarism at its core. It therefore prejudges, so the criticism runs, a problem which man has been unable to solve throughout history – whether we are free or determined.

The rejoinder to this criticism is obvious. Free-will versus determinism is indeed a metaphysical problem, one that can never be solved as a matter of evidence. To grant human beings free will clearly implies a major assumption; but it is just as much of an assumption to see man as completely determined. The reasons for preferring the former assumption are first of all pragmatic. It so happens that positivistic psychology has palpably failed to create a science of any real benefit to the human race. Not only that, but some of its consequences for the conduct of human affairs are, as we shall see in later chapters, distinctly unpleasant. To my mind, however, the ultimate justification for preferring the assumption of freedom is that this is the natural view of man. I mean by this that in nature man experiences himself as able to choose; this is a basic fact of existence. Interestingly enough, people who make an outright denial of this freedom for themselves run the grave risk of being labelled by a psychiatrist as schizophrenic. Paradoxically then, if psychology is to be a natural science in the true sense of the word, it must begin by assuming man to be what he experiences himself as being in the natural world – capable of choosing, planning, and executing his own actions.

A slightly more sophisticated objection to a science of persons is that by allowing man freedom, even of a limited kind, science is thereby made impossible because, if man is free, there is no way of predicting what he will do and therefore no chance of describing his behaviour in lawful terms. In order to reply to this criticism it is necessary to introduce the idea that man is essentially a *rule-following animal*. Harré (1974) points out that in human social conduct there is a great deal of regularity. For example, in the USA, 'thank you' is followed almost inevitably by the reply 'you're welcome', with a predictability found rarely even in physics. However, nobody would seriously consider describing this situation by saying that one utterance 'causes' the other. The regularity is there because both parties to the interaction are following rules relating to social etiquette. The point I wish to make though is that one is still free to ignore such conventions and break the rules, provided one is prepared to run the risk of being thought ill-mannered and loutish. Therefore, it is easy to reconcile the assumption that man is free to choose with the fact of lawful regularities in human behaviour. This is not the cause and effect lawfulness of the billiard table, but a lawfulness based on the principle that man self-consciously monitors his behaviour according to a set of rules.

Let me illustrate the task of the scientist under this rule-following model of man by employing a well-known example. The scientist is in the situation of a foreigner watching a cricket match for the first time. Initially our friend is very puzzled; the players appear to be acting in quite arbitrary and mysterious ways. Gradually he begins to see repeated patterns in what is happening and may begin to form hypotheses to account for these patterns. These hypotheses will, in fact, be guesses about the rules of cricket, and having made a guess our friend will then see whether the hypothesized rule is borne out in further play, whether any exceptions to the rule can be accommodated by modifications to it, or whether it has to be scrapped and a new rule proposed. And so on.

Although I hope that this example is helpful in expounding the rule-following model of man, I would not wish it to be taken too literally in certain important respects. In the first place, our visitor is more accurately in the position of the cultural anthropologist, attempting to make sense of the strange customs of some newly discovered tribe. The psychologist, however, will usually be concerned to describe rules existing in his own culture. Secondly, I would not want to give the impression that all the rules we live by are analogous to the *formal rules* of a game. If this were the case, psychology would give way to sociology, since it is one of the tasks of sociology to describe the *cultural norms* by which men live. These, like the formal rules of cricket, are important in understanding why men behave as they do, but, to extend the metaphor, a mere knowledge of the rules will not explain everything that is happening in a particular game of cricket – for example, the performances of individual players or the personal relationships among them. In brief, the psychologist must concern himself with rule-following because an individual person is by definition responsible for his actions; in other words, he forms plans and executes them by monitoring his performance according to rules. To account for how these plans and rules arise is one of the principal tasks of a science of persons but, however exactly they arise, it must necessarily be the case that they are negotiated *between* people in social interaction, including of course early interactions between parent and child. I would prefer to leave a discussion of the demarcation of psychology from other disciplines to a later section, but let us establish here that *a science of persons incorporating the rule-following model of man must be a social psychology.*

I said before that the freedom granted to man by a science of persons need only be a limited freedom. It is necessary to include the limitations in the model because it would be foolish to assert that there were no constraints on human behaviour. These constraints are best thought of as being two kinds – biological and sociological.

To take the biological constraints first, it is clear that hormones, reflexes, and other aspects of biological make-up (including perhaps unconscious 'wishes') exercise some determining influence on what we do. If I have taken some kind of drug, for example, a full explanation of my behaviour will have to take that fact into account. What is essential for the reader to grasp, however, is that man is unique among forms of life for being able to *transcend* these determining influences. In virtue of his self-awareness and use of language, he is able to construct his world, represent it to himself, and frame his actions accordingly.

The same kind of reasoning applies to sociological constraints upon us, the way in which our understanding of the world is shaped by the social institutions of the culture we live in. There is much talk these days of the need to overcome 'conditioning', in a sense of that word which is similar to what we were discussing here, the influence of the prevailing culture upon us. Thus it is said, for example, that we are conditioned to accept particular kinds of ways of living together and particular kinds of gender-roles. The very fact that people can speak of overcoming their conditioning argues for the transcendent view of man I am supporting here.

A general way of summing all this up is to say that our freedom is limited by the degree to which we have transcended, in the construction of our experience, the biological and sociological determinants of our behaviour. It might be argued that the very task of psychology is to assist people in that endeavour.

Facts

Recently, Broadbent (1973) has written *In Defence of Empirical Psychology*. Broadbent, an avowed behaviourist and one of the most influential men in British psychology, is concerned to defend empirical psychology, which he equates with behaviourism, from recent radical attacks on it. He believes that, if successful, these attacks will lead to mere polemic between hostile dogmas. As we shall see, however, Broadbent's defence is misplaced, being based on certain misunderstandings both as to the nature of recent criticisms of behaviourism and, apparently, as to the proper meaning of *empiricism*.

As Broadbent rightly points out, 'empirical psychology' has come to mean two things. First, it affirms a belief in the experimental method in psychology. Secondly, it describes a view of human nature which asserts that its chief characteristic is its modifiability through learning. This second meaning is closer to the way in which philosophers use the term 'empiricism'. This refers to the belief that all, or most, of our knowledge of the world is arrived at through experience. The opposite view, which is known as *rationalism*, refers to the contrary belief that our knowledge is chiefly *a priori*: that is, prior to, and independent of, experience. Now, whichever of these two philosophical views is ultimately correct, science is always empirical; the very activity of doing science automatically assumes that it is concerned with questions of fact, with knowledge arrived at through experience, and not with knowledge arrived at by deductive reasoning or any other category of knowledge independent of experience. Thus, few critics of behaviourism would dream of denying that psychology should be empirical in this proper sense of the term, as Broadbent suggests they do. The point of their criticism, which is missed by Broadbent, is that there is more than one way of being empirical, that empirical methods are not limited to laboratory methods copied from physics. Furthermore, in equating empirical psychology with behaviourism, Broadbent implies that the only 'facts' open to an empirical science of psychology are facts as prescribed by behaviourism. To repeat, nobody is denying that psychology must be based on facts; the disagreement is about the nature of those facts, what they represent, and how they are to be used and interpreted.

One misuse of facts which recent critics have emphasized is peculiar to British psychology. This is the idea that psychology can be done by merely collecting a lot of different facts and adding them up until, in some mysterious fashion, they amount to a science. Thus, the aspiring psychologist is advised to postpone theorizing, to stop worrying about what he is doing and why, and just go out there and do experiments. If enough of these experiments are done, it is implied, we can ultimately arrive at a complete understanding of behaviour.

What is wrong with this view of science, which is best described as *naive empiricism*? The answer is that it entails a complete misunderstanding of how scientific knowledge grows. There is no such thing as a 'fact' which does not require some degree of interpretation on the part of the observer; in other words, facts have meanings. The only way to ensure that the meaning of a fact increases our knowledge rather than adds to our confusion is to place it within the

25

framework of a theory. The alternative, to experiment randomly in the absence of theory, can only lead to a jumble of unrelated facts and untranslatable meanings, without system or order.

I have perhaps already spent too long on this issue, since to say that psychology must be theoretical is by no means necessarily a radical line of argument. After all, the most ambitious attempt yet made in psychology at a complete theory is Hull's hypothetico-deductive system, which failed lamentably to reduce the complexities of human behaviour to the antics of rats in mazes, but which, along the way, had a damaging influence on psychology for more than a decade. To reiterate the main point, however, *a collection of facts will never by itself constitute a science of psychology.*

From these broad considerations concerning the nature of science in general, let us now turn to a more specific examination of behaviourism and the kinds of facts delimited by this conception of psychology. As the reader will know, the chief argument for behaviourism is that if psychology is to be a science it can deal only with what is observable. Behaviour is observable, but mind or consciousness is unobservable. Hence, we can never make reliable and repeatable observations of another person's mind and, hence, subjective experience can have no place in a science of psychology. At face value this argument may appear plausible but a moment's reflection will reveal it to rest on a logical absurdity.

The behaviourists say, in effect, that we can never have reliable knowledge of another's experience. The absurdity of this argument lies in the fact that if this were true, science itself would become impossible, because the observations made by scientists are part of their experience. Since experience has already been defined as private, it would be impossible ever to share scientific observations and the entire enterprise of science would crumble at its inception. There is a philosophical term for this mistaken idea that we all live in completely closed, isolated worlds inaccessible to each other; it is called *solipsism.* As Sartre (1957) has put it: 'Behaviourism is solipsism as a working hypothesis.'

Is it true then that we can have knowledge of other minds? Not only can we, but our very use of language shows that we cannot avoid at least attempting it. The case for behaviourism is sometimes supported by the following example. It is not permissible to say 'the dog is sad', since this would be to make a statement about the dog's private experience which is inaccessible to us. All we can say is that 'the dog whines', since this is an objective statement. Let us look at this example a little more closely and see how objective the last statement really is. Surely, the fact that we describe the dog as whining makes an immediate reference to the dog's experience. If we were to be truly 'objective' about the dog's behaviour we could only describe the noise emitted by it in terms of pitch, tone, and loudness. But to do this would be to strip our 'objective fact' of all content; no amount of description in terms of physical characteristics would ever add up to what we understand by a whine. Thus, in order to make an intelligible observation about the dog's behaviour, we must take into account its *meaning*, and this meaning will reflect the subjective experience accompanying the animal's behaviour.

Of course, no one would seriously recommend the study of the subjective experiences of dogs. This study would be severely hampered by the fact that our subjects cannot talk to us and the force of the example given above is to show that, even in this case, behaviour has meaning. In the case of human beings, information about their thoughts, feelings, etc., is gained simply by talking to them. The fact that we can understand what they mean when they talk about their thoughts and feelings shows that statements about subjective states are not qualitatively different from statements about overt behaviour, as regards the possibilty of agreement about them. To sum up, the distinction claimed by behaviourists between statements about objective, observable events and statements about subjective, unobservable events is invalid.

I have criticized the behaviouristic interpretation of facts by arguing that observations about behaviour are always meaningful. In general terms, it is this area of meaning which behaviourism and later forms of positivistic psychology cannot handle. Let us now consider both sides of the behaviourist equation – stimulus and response – in the light of this question of meaning. The reader may, if she likes, substitute the more modern terms 'input' and 'output'. The same considerations apply to most of what follows.

Previously I pointed out that it is inherent in man to interpret his experience and represent it to himself. One might say that man was a creature who was able to construct theories about himself and the world and act upon them. It is now time to introduce an important notion in the radical critique of psychology, the notion that a science of psychology must be *reflexive*. For psychology to be reflexive, I mean that any theory of human behaviour must be able to explain how theories of human behaviour come about, because the making of theories is part of the human behaviour that the theory sets out in the first place to explain. This idea may take a little getting used to and I had better elaborate on it. Philosophers of science would agree that the activity of scientists in theorizing, experimenting, and observing, etc., is not different *in kind* from the ordinary activity of other men and women and, indeed, from the activity of scientists when they are not wearing scientific hats. Scientific activity is, after all, human activity and, conversely, ordinary human activity can conveniently be seen as a less systematic and articulate version of what scientists do. So the psychologist is in the very peculiar position of having to make observations about observers, to experiment with experimenters and theorize about theorizers. George Kelly solved this conundrum in a very economical fashion by proposing the model of '*man the scientist*'. Kelly's *Personal Construct Theory* is concerned to provide ways of discovering how individual people make sense of their experience and use it to deal with the world. For present purposes, let us merely note that an acid test of any psychological theory is the question, whether it is capable of explaining its own creation. The reader will find that no behaviourist or otherwise reductionist theory can pass this test.

But what has all this to do with the behaviourist interpretation of facts? It is that, as these considerations demonstrate, *there is no such thing as a stimulus*. The notion of a stimulus requires that an event has a standard effect on all those who are subject to it. But, as we have seen, man is a creature who makes an interpretation of what happens to him, so that we can never be sure that what is a stimulus for one person is the same stimulus for another, or is the same stimulus that the experimenter intended it to be. To take a trivial example, if the experimenter presents me with a 'stressful' stimulus by requiring me to perform rapid arithmetical calculations, it may be that for some perverse reason I find the experience quite enjoyable and not stressful at all. Stranger things have been known.

The same argument applies to that important class of stimuli, the reinforcers. Again, it is always assumed that some reinforcers are positive and some negative. This means, whatever scholastic hedging is done on the issue, that some are rewarding and some are punishing. An appropriate task for psychology would be to discover why one individual is rewarded in some ways and another in different ways. A solution would require a study of the meanings the events have for the particular individual in question.

Let us turn to the response side of the behaviourist equation. I have already referred to the fact that human behaviour is typically meaningful as an expression of the behaver. The point I wish to make now is slightly different. The term 'response' implies that something is done as a result of something that happened in the past, the event that is responded to. This is part of the mechanistic model of man we considered earlier. The alternative advanced by a psychology of persons would stress that human action is always directed towards *the future*. This is another way to see behaviour as meaningful. A movement acquires meaning and becomes an action by being seen as part of a sequence of actions which together go to make up a plan, or complete act. I am in a shop and execute the following movements: I put my hand in my pocket, pull out some change, and place some of it on the counter. How may we understand these movements – as 'responses' mechanically elicited by past events? Surely not. The best way to understand them is to see them as fitting into the larger sequence of movements called 'buying a loaf of bread'. My behaviour is unintelligible outside the context of the future events of my taking the bread out of the shop and eating some of it for my tea. Most human behaviour is meaningful in this sense simply because it is *intentional behaviour*.

The idea of reflexivity is also useful here. The reader will no doubt have been instructed that the object of doing experiments is to predict their outcomes. Obviously what is being predicted are future events. So, if some people called scientists can attempt to predict the future, and act on that basis, why can't everybody else? The answer is they can and

29

do. This anticipatory nature of human action is an essential ingredient of the aforementioned Personal Construct Theory (see D3).

To conclude this discussion of facts, I want to introduce another aspect of meaning which positivistic psychologies cannot accommodate. Here we shall be concerned with the failure of academic psychology, with its individualistic bias, to incorporate in its view of man his essentially social nature, and in this I do not want to exclude most of what currently passes as social psychology.

Take the example of someone driving a car who wishes to turn right and sticks her hand out of the car window to indicate her intention to do so. Again, let us consider how best to explain this action. I would submit that no explanation which takes only the individual into account could ever tell us why the driver made this particular movement. Certainly, no explanation which attempted to reduce the behaviour in question to lower levels could ever succeed in explaining its symbolic significance as a gesture, and this might be a convenient time to expose *the fallacy of reductionism*, or at least one way of doing so. Imagine that we were able to provide a complete and accurate description of what happened in the brain when the movement was initiated: the passage of an electrical impulse along the neurone, the consequent contraction of muscles, the kinaesthetic feedback this produced and so on and so forth. We might thus be able to explain all the physical movements which go to make up the gesture. But could an explanation in these terms ever tell us that extending one's right arm from a car window has a particular meaning in the culture: 'I intend to turn right'? Clearly not. The attempt to reduce the phenomenon to a more 'fundamental' level of explanation merely succeeds in destroying the meaning essential to an understanding of it.

Having established that the piece of behaviour in question cannot be reduced to a neurophysiological level, we must now go further and say that it is impossible to reduce it to any individualistic kind of explanation whatever. The fact that the arm signal means what it does exists as a *social fact*, independently of any individual understandings of it. To explain why the driver acted as she did, we need to take into account not only her understanding of the meaning of the gesture, but her further understanding that other drivers understand it also and will themselves act on that understanding. We could not imagine someone on a desert island making a gesture similar to the example we are considering, because such a gesture would have no meaning for anyone else. Thus, the behaviour in question is best described as *symbolic interaction*. The behaviour has symbolic significance as a communication *between* individuals, in a way which rules out the possibility of understanding it *within* individuals. The same is true of any human behaviour which involves shared meanings and expectations, including of course that vital area of human activity, language.

The upshot of this for social psychology is that if it is to be truly social, it must focus on the way in which meanings, expectations, and rules of action are negotiated between people, rather than present the positivistic picture of isolated individuals merely 'responding' to each other in a social context, as it tends to do now. In short, social psychology must undertake a study of *shared experience*. This desideratum is most adequately met by the theoretical tradition of symbolic interactionism in sociology, following from the work of G. H. Mead. It is a sobering thought for psychologists that the only social psychology worthy of that title is predominantly the work of people trained in sociology.

Methods
Perhaps the reader will already be able to guess the more obvious criticisms of experimental methods in psychology. Under the influence of positivism, psychologists have attempted to squeeze the study of human life into a laboratory situation where it becomes unrecognizably different from its naturally occurring form.

In the first place, positivism dictates that everything in the experimental setting be made as simple as possible, so that hopefully unequivocal conclusions may be drawn. Thus, traditionally, the independent variables are restricted to one and the dependent variable, the subject's behaviour, is made as banal as possible – pressing buttons, saying 'yes' or 'no', ticking boxes in a questionnaire, and so forth – so that unambiguous observations may be made of it. Then simple links may be drawn, after the fashion of the mechanistic conception

31

of causation, between antecedent and consequent events.

The fallacy here is to believe that the complexity of human psychology can be reduced in this way or, conversely, that adding up these simple results will ever amount to a picture of what human life is really like. The fact is that, because of the rich meanings which are inextricably interlaced in human behaviour and experience, the complexity with which we are confronted in everyday life exists *in its own right and at its own level*. The attempt to chop it up into little bits, into elementary connections between artificial events, succeeds only in restricting the range of behaviour which is open to the subject, to the exclusion of behaviour which might have any relevance to real life outside the laboratory. What follows is the sheer triviality of experimental findings and the justifiable disappointment of the 'layman', the alleged beneficiary of all this effort, when he is informed of them. The alternative to the laboratory in psychology is to study human life *in its natural setting*. Rather than the subject come to the experimenter, the experimenter should go to the subject. This does not necessarily mean that we must abandon the virtues of the scientific method; it means only that we must tailor those methods to the appropriate context of inquiry. A useful analogy here is with the revolution in the study of animal behaviour effected by the ethologists. By taking their studies out of the laboratory into the field and adjusting their methods accordingly, Lorenz, Tinbergen, and others began the study of animal behaviour in the natural world. What we need, if you like, is *an ethology of human life*.

A different sort of criticism of the experimental method is contained in the idea that *a psychological experiment is a social situation*. As we have seen, human social behaviour is to a large extent regulated by rules of conduct and mutual expectations of the interactants. Exactly the same considerations apply in the laboratory. Two recent lines of evidence appear to demonstrate that these rules and expectations are often the most important determinants of the results produced. Orne (1962) has referred to what he calls the 'demand characteristics' of experiments; the subject of the experiment is able to guess from the experimenter's behaviour what is expected of her and may or may not decide to conform to these expectations. Rosenthal (1966) demonstrated the other side of the coin by showing how in 'experimenter bias' the experimenter unwittingly suggests to the subject how she should behave. The importance of these demonstrations is made clear by recalling once more the reflexive nature of psychological science. Since the 'subject' is herself in the business of forming hypotheses and making predictions about behaviour, the way she acts in the experiment will be determined largely by the interaction going on between herself and the experimenter. Let me put it another way, to make clear the difference between experiments in psychology and those in the physical sciences on which they are based. Let us imagine that a chemist, after having poured one acid into another to observe the resultant combination, decides to masturbate while the experiment is in progress. Now, this may be highly unusual behaviour, but it is difficult to see how the experimenter's actions could possibly affect the result of the experiment. Could the same be said if the same thing happened in a psychological experiment? This rather dramatic example makes the point I set out to prove, that experiments in psychology are primarily social situations. More specifically, they are social situations involving strangers, and it might be suggested that the main kind of knowledge gleaned from years of experimentation with human subjects is information about how strangers interact in the highly artificial and unusual social setting of the psychological experiment. Even if the reader regards this as going too far, she should bear in mind that experiments are never done with passive 'subjects' but only with active 'participants'. One of the best ways of discovering the absurdity and futility of most psychological experimentation is to serve as a 'subject' oneself, and this exercise is highly recommended.

We have now reached the final part of this discussion of methods in psychology, the presentation of the main alternative to current experimental methods, the phenomenological method. I shall have space for a brief discussion only of an extremely complex subject. The phenomenological tradition is usually dated back to the work of the German philosopher, Edmund Husserl, although I shall not be concerned here with philosophical phenomenology but with the phenomenological method as applied to psychology.

The reader may recall that in the previous section on facts I implied that all scientific knowledge, and indeed all knowledge whatever, is ultimately grounded in experience. The phenomenological method differs from behaviouristic methods in that the facts towards which it is directed are not the facts of behaviour, but the facts of experience. The catchphrase of phenomenology is 'back to the data', where the word 'data' stands for its correct and original meaning of *that which is given* in experience. The method is concerned with enabling us to inquire into our experience, and that of others, by excluding the biases of our preconceptions about it. It tells us how to put aside our assumptions so that we may arrive at what is essential and indubitable in our immediate experience without distortion from traditional notions and received ideas as to its nature.

It is important not to confuse the phenomenological method, as I have described it, with introspection. As the reader will know, Watson and the early behaviourists rejected introspection as a method because the introspectionists could not agree amongst themselves about their findings and seemed to have no way of resolving their disputes. (Later events showed that the behaviourists were in no better a position as regards these matters than those they scorned.) However, the failure of the introspectionists was due to their embarking on the wrong task. Influenced by the success of the analytical chemistry of their time, they believed that they could analyse mind into simple, irreducible units similar to the basic elements of chemistry – the influence of positivism again. It was about what those elements of mind were that they disagreed. The mistake they made is one which should by now be familar. It is not possible to reduce experience in this way without destroying its meaning. Phenomenology approaches experience as a whole, does not attempt to analyse it into parts, and regards meaning as central to it.

Possibly the most important aspect of phenomenological psychology is known as *the phenomenology of the other person*. In different ways during this chapter the reader has been introduced to an idea which is completely antithetical to the philosophical basis of modern academic psychology rooted in behaviourism. This is the idea that experience is, or can be, shared. In their concept of *intersubjectivity* the phenomenologists stress that we may have direct access to each other's experience through shared meaning. We may enter

34

into the world of the other and know what it feels like to be there; we may reconstruct others' experience of the world and share their thoughts, feelings, and emotions. Perhaps it would be wiser not to argue this point further but simply appeal to the reader's own experience of personal relationships and ask whether she can confirm what is being claimed.

The chief historical influence of phenomenology has been upon the European philosophical movement of existentialism. This movement has provided some invaluable contributions to a psychology of experience which have been shamefully neglected by British and American psychologists. More recently, phenomenology and existentialism have had some direct influence on psychology in America, and have contributed significantly to the movement known as *the third force*. This loose and wide-ranging movement, associated with the names of Carl Rogers, Abraham Maslow, and Sidney Jourard, acquires its title from its rejection of both psychoanalysis and behaviourism, and its desire to establish a truly *humanistic psychology* in opposition to both. Its main object of study is 'the self', and its primary emphasis is upon personal growth and development. In the past few years, the impact of the third force is beginning to be felt in Britain, albeit outside academic departments of psychology. I shall have more to say about the implications of this movement later in the book.

Finally, a quotation from David Matza (1969) will serve as an eloquent plea for phenomenological methods, supported by a humanistic and naturalistic perspective, in human science. Matza, whose own work with delinquents represents a good example of the phenomenological approach, also echoes several major themes of this chapter:

Man participates in meaningful activity. He creates his reality, and that of the world around him, actively and strenuously. Man naturally – not supernaturally – transcends the existential realms in which the conceptions of cause, force, and reactivity are easily applicable. Accordingly, a view that conceives man as object, methods that probe human behavior without concerning themselves with the meaning of behavior, cannot be regarded as naturalist. Such views and methods are the very opposite of naturalism because they have molested in advance the phenomenon to

35

be studied. Naturalism when applied to the study of man has no choice but to conceive man as subject precisely because naturalism claims fidelity to the empirical world. In the empirical world, man is subject and not object, except when he is likened to one by himself or by another subject. Naturalism must choose the subjective view, and consequently it must combine the scientific method with the distinctive tools of humanism – experience, intuition, and empathy. Naturalism has no other choice because its philosophical commitment is neither to objectivity nor subjectivity, neither to scientific method nor humanist sensibility. Its only commitment is fidelity to the phenomenon under consideration. Thus, in the study of man, there is no antagonism between naturalism and a repudiation of the objective view, nor a contradiction between naturalism and the humane methods of experience, reason, intuition, and empathy. Naturalism in the study of man is a disciplined and rigorous humanism.

Towards a proper science of psychology

It is now time to draw together some of the threads of this chapter and reiterate a few simple points. I started by saying that positivistic psychology uses science to dehumanize man and it should now be clear what this means. Positivistic psychology is a psychology which *reduces man to a thing* and thereby destroys all that is essentially human in him. As McLeod (1964) has remarked, the simplest way of reducing a person to a thing is to shoot him, but this is generally frowned on as being unscientific. I hope the reader will not consider it too extravagant a metaphor if I say that positivistic psychology murders the human beings it studies.

It should also be clear that what is being advocated here is not the abandonment of science. This is often a false characterization of radical views put forward by the more conservatively minded. On the contrary, the radical perspective of academic psychology prizes a truly scientific psychology more highly than the positivistic perspective to which it is opposed. That is why it claims that it is *unscientific* to treat people as things, and that is why it urges that we must strive towards a proper science of psychology, one that is appropriate to its subject matter – man. Obviously there are great difficulties in the way of this undertaking and I believe that it has only just got started. But the fact that it will be difficult is no reason to shirk it. Indeed, psychology must undertake such a task if it is to create a science of any real benefit to the human race.

What will this proper science of psychology, or science of persons, look like? It is possible to describe a few broad distinguishing features. First, it will not be a psychology which can be reduced to physiology; it will be *discontinuous* from the physical sciences, including the physical sciences of man. The part of what is now called psychology which employs physiological concepts may be a legitimate area of study, but its object will be to increase our understanding of the brain and nervous system and not of meaningful human action. The study of movements is physiology; psychology is the study of actions.

Secondly, a science of persons will be discontinuous from the biological sciences of animal behaviour because the human situation contains features which make it qualitatively different from other forms of life. Man's self-awareness, his use of language, and his consequent ability to represent the world to himself and thereby transcend it, make the study of man an inquiry *sui generis* – of its own kind.

Thirdly, as I said previously, the science of persons will be essentially a social psychology, regarding man's social nature as a basic characteristic of the species. The study of human action is identical with the study of human interaction. This is no place to enter into a discussion of where and how a line may be drawn between the science of persons and the science of sociology, except to say that I believe it can be drawn.

Finally, a science of persons will be a science which is truly reflexive. This means, amongst other things, that it will not be a science done by some people, the experts, about other people, the non-experts, for the benefit of some other people, those with the power to employ psychologists. It will be a science done by some people about all of us for the benefit of everybody. But here we anticipate the next chapter.

Concluding remarks

I have tried in this chapter to describe the main features of positivism and its effect on psychology and to present some aspects of what might be called a radical academic psychology. This presentation has been necessarily brief, selective, and highly condensed, and I can only hope that the reader will pursue the further reading listed at the end of the book. Nor have I tried to be systematic in the presentation of alternative standpoints to positivistic psychology; that would be a task far beyond the scope of this introduction to the area. If the chapter has succeeded it has raised more questions than it has answered.

But there is one set of questions which have only been hinted at. What is the attraction of positivism? Why is it that human beings have so consistently been described for scientific purposes as if they were things? How has this come about and for whose benefit is it? To these questions we now turn.

3
Values and ideology

I spent the last chapter trying to reveal some of the inadequacies of a psychology which treats persons as things. I obviously want to say that such a psychology can never provide a satisfactory account of human life. In this chapter I want to go on to show in what ways the employment of this psychology is dangerous and ultimately harmful to the way we live. But before doing this, it might be as well to clear up an apparent contradiction which may have occurred to the reader. How can I say in the same breath that positivistic psychology is both inadequate and harmful? If it is wrong, why worry about it? If on the other hand it is dangerous, must there not be some power in its arguments? The short answer to these questions is that positivistic psychology can be both wrong and dangerous because *its function in society is primarily ideological*. We need now to examine in more detail what this bald statement means.

Science and values

Ironically enough, the discipline of psychology itself can be seen as providing strong supportive evidence for the thesis that science reflects the values and interests of the scientists who do it, and is not the strictly objective, value-free enterprise that positivism takes it for. For example, the 'new look'

39

in perception in the late 1940s demonstrated how our interests, beliefs, and motivations have predictable influences on what we perceive. Subsequently, a whole movement in British psychology was devoted to showing how what we attended to was systematically biased towards some things and away from others (see A4). And the notion of 'cognitive dissonance' might be crudely summarized in the assertion of how difficult we find it to accept evidence which is in conflict with what we already believe (see B1 and B3). In these and a number of other ways, psychology has confirmed the commonsense notion that our cherished beliefs, our preconceived ideas, and basic value-judgements on life distort our understanding of the world. There is no reason to think the same is not true of our scientific understanding, especially in the more emotionally loaded sciences of man. Science is done by men and women and the findings of psychology must therefore apply to it.

It might be objected against this that the methods of science are specifically designed to minimize the danger of this subjective bias creeping into our observations. This is true, although, as I tried to show in the last chapter, the ideal of simple, unambiguous observations on the model of the physical sciences is an impossible target for psychology owing to the meaningful nature of behaviour. In any case, the thesis that psychology rests on values is less concerned with the influence of these values on direct observations than with higher order issues. These issues derive partly from the social organization of science but more importantly from unavoidable features of psychology as science.

First, the necessary complexities of the statistical methods used in psychology (see A8) make it very difficult to arrive at genuinely repeatable observations. For every finding in psychology, there seems always to be a contradictory finding. Out of the confusion thus engendered, what eventually emerges as established fact is likely to be influenced by what the scientific establishment prefers to regard as fact. Secondly, the proliferation of concepts, theories, and distinct theoretical languages makes straightforward interpretation of these facts almost an impossibility. For every hypothetical interpretation of a finding, there seems always to be an alternative hypothesis which can be made to fit the facts equally well. Again, the conquering hypothesis may well be the one which is most palatable to those with power.

Thirdly, there is the important question of the way in which the attention of psychologists is directed towards certain problems to the exclusion of other problems and relevant observations. What is regarded as a problem in psychology – for example, how to sort out the educational wheat from the chaff – and the concepts which result from a consideration of that problem – for example, the concept of IQ – may be determined by whose interests are served by a solution to it. Fourthly, underlying most empirical areas of inquiry are certain assumptions which are not themselves a matter of evidence but depend upon basic preferences about how society should be organized and how we should live in it. For instance, the language of normal–abnormal, adaptive–maladaptive, etc., which is central to a certain influential type of psychology, usually implies the unspoken assumption that normality in our society and adaptability to it are a good thing.

Finally, and possibly of most importance, the 'model of man' adopted by psychology, the kind of creature man is taken to be, cannot be a matter of evidence but must necessarily imply some value or preference for one view of man against another. The effect of this and of the other particular ways in which values influence the science of psychology will be illustrated at various points throughout the book.

A more general way of understanding how science may be said to rest on values is contained in the idea that scientific knowledge is *pragmatic* knowledge, in the widest sense of the word. This means that in the last analysis, the justification and validity of the physical sciences rest on their capacity to allow us to control the physical world and modify it according to agreed principles of human benefit. This in itself entails a value-judgement, but one which is hardly contentious – that our increased mastery over the physical environment, in a way which works for the benefit of our race, is a desirable event. When we apply the same kind of reasoning to psychology and other human sciences, however, the issues are far less clear. If we define psychology positivistically as the prediction and control of behaviour, all sorts of interesting questions begin to emerge. While the control of nature may not be controversial, the control of men and women surely is. To what ends should

41

this control be directed? Who is to do the controlling and who is to be controlled? And how is this to be decided? The reader will readily appreciate that these are *traditionally political questions*, invoking immediately some of the most vital statements of value we are called upon to make in life.

It is a common misinterpretation of the radical critique of psychology that it aims to drag politics into psychology. It cannot be emphasized enough that what is really being said, and what in a sense the radical critique is devoted to demonstrating, is that *political issues are inherent in psychology*.

Having established, I trust, that psychology depends ultimately on the values of its practitioners, I now want to show how these values systematically distort psychology in a particular direction. In brief, this systematic bias and this distortion serve *the function of preserving the status quo*; that is, of assisting in the prevention of radical social change. To understand how this comes about, we need to examine the concept of ideology.

What is ideology?

Although the term has been employed in a number of different senses, 'ideology' is primarily a Marxist concept. The key to its understanding is the proposition that our experience and behaviour are shaped in large part by our social circumstances; the sense we make of the world is usually a product of the culture we live in. In particular, the specifically Marxist thesis is that our understanding of the world reflects the economic relationships existing in society. Thus, in a capitalist society, the ideas and actions of those who stand to benefit most from that society will have the effect of supporting and maintaining it. Put at its simplest, *ideology is disguised self-interest*.

This self-interest however is not something of which its exponents are necessarily aware, and ideology does not refer to an overt 'conspiracy' on the part of capitalists to prolong their exploitation. Rather, the exploitation is protected by a system of illusions which serve to make it appear legitimate and disguise its true nature. The exploiters are just as much victims of these illusions as those they exploit, since their self-interest also prevents them from realizing the character of their exploitative relationships with others. Thus the origin of ideology is not the small minority who constitute the capitalist class, but the economic system which generates the divisions in society that the ideology serves to obscure. Nor should we think of the production of ideology as being confined to the capitalist class. In Marx's time the main vehicle of ideology was religion, and it was therefore the priests who were chiefly instrumental in persuading people to be satisfied with their lot. Nowadays, it is often argued, it is the role of science and scientists to glorify and hence make acceptable the increasingly industrial, technological society in which we live. In doing so, science serves the interests of those who control the sources of wealth and power in our society. In addition, of course, the scientists themselves do not do badly out of the system and therefore become unwitting apologists for it.

Our understanding of the way ideology works in advanced, industrial society has been greatly increased by the writings of Herbert Marcuse. In his celebrated book *One Dimensional Man*, Marcuse (1964) showed how new forms of social control have been perfected whose effect is to obliterate criticism and protest. These social controls are based upon the capacity of technology to satisfy basic material needs and then create new, false needs for other forms of consumption and material possessions in order that it may continue to satisfy these. Thus, ideology in our society is a process of persuading people to accept a definition of their existence in which they are transformed into passive consumers without responsibility for their own lives and in which, in return for obeying the decisions of others, they are rewarded by the increased consumption of goods they have come to believe they need. By means of this 'voluntary and comfortable servitude', not only is dissent from the system stifled but human creative possibilities cease to exist and man becomes veritably 'one-dimensional'.

For our immediate purposes then, we will need to observe how, amongst other things, positivism and its form of psychology assist in the maintenance of the technological, consumer society and help to neutralize dissent from it.

One recent commentator (Kolakowski, 1972) on logical empiricism or logical positivism has concluded thus:

> Logical empiricism is the product of a specific culture, one in which technological efficiency is regarded as the highest value, the culture we usually call 'technocratic'. It is a technocratic ideology in the guise of an anti-ideological, scientific view of the world purged of value-judgements.

Kolakowski's reason for reaching this conclusion, that logical positivism is founded upon hidden technocratic values, is that the principle of verification, central to positivist doctrine, boils down on close examination to a question of what is practically useful. This can only be culturally defined as what is useful to advanced, industrial society. Therefore, psychology positivistically conceived is, as I suggested in the last section, a psychology in the service of organized capitalism.

Speaking of radical positivism, the most influential branch of positivism which rules out value-judgements as meaningless, Kolakowski writes:

> Positivism in this sense is the escapist's design for living, a life voluntarily cut off from participation in anything that cannot be correctly formulated. The language it imposes exempts us from the duty of speaking up in life's most important conflicts ...

In other words, this kind of positivism is an intellectual cop-out. Several critics of positivism have suggested that its influence upon intellectuals between the wars contributed to the rise of fascism, owing to its justification for *le trahison des clercs* – the unwillingness of intellectuals, including scientists, to take sides in political struggles.

Philosophical positivism as a whole may be seen as ideological because it is historically passive and neutral. I mean by this that in its cult of 'the fact', positivism accepts the facts presented to it in any given society as being *the only possible reality* and can never envisage these historically contingent facts as being subject to change. In doing so, positivism puts the seal of scientific authority and finality on that which is

given in the particular society it finds itself. Its function therefore is essentially conservative, to preserve what is there in
the form of 'fact' and to prevent question or change.

Ways in which positivistic psychology is ideological

There are a few obvious ways in which modern psychology is
ideological. For example, the use of psychology in market research and advertising, with the aim of gulling people into
buying trash or preferring one identical product to another,
bolsters the consumerism necessary to advanced capitalism
(see F6). The employment of psychologists by government to
refine methods of extracting information (as in the use of
sensory deprivation as torture), or to develop more suitable
methods of crowd control, is clearly calculated to resist any
movement towards social change. Hardly less obvious is the
use of intelligence testing to justify the oppression of blacks
and other minority groups. However, although I would agree
that these perversions of psychology should be resisted as
much as possible on every possible occasion, it is more important for us at this point to uncover less obviously ideological
aspects of the discipline. These arise not from the applications
of psychology, as in the few examples above, but are embedded
in the corpus of modern psychology itself.

This more obscure ideological content of psychology follows from the inadequacies I discussed in the last chapter –
the denial of human action, the negation of meaning and the
suppression of the social dimension from descriptions of
human affairs. We have to add to this a shortcoming which I
mentioned for the first time in the present chapter (see p. 44)
– the inability of positivism to comprehend society historically.
Although I do not claim that the list is exhaustive, there follow five related ways in which positivistic psychology serves a
hidden ideological purpose.

Reification
This word refers to what is perhaps the main topic of this
book, the transformation of persons into things. In describing
the ideological content of the process of reification, Ingleby
(1972) writes:

eifying model of human nature, by definition, presents as less than they really are (or could be): to the extent that a society requires men (or a certain proportion of them) to be thing-like in their work, orientation, thinking and experiencing, such a model will constitute both a reflection and a reinforcement of that society (reinforcing because men tend to become what they are told they *are*). If labour is mechanical, it is convenient that those who have to do it should think of themselves as a species of machine: if freedom of choice, imagination, the pursuit of untried goals and experiences are seen as threats to a sacrosanct 'social structure', then man should learn that he is a species of simple computer, a 'limited capacity information channel', incapable by definition of creating such goals and such meanings.

Here Ingleby shows very clearly how the 'model of man' put over by psychology has vital consequences for how people think of themselves and others; psychology is unlike the physical sciences in that the object of its study is capable of understanding what is being said about it and may actually accept what it is told. In this sense psychology has, as Ingleby points out, a 'mythic' function; it describes an image of man which fits perfectly the *alienation* of man necessary to capitalism. 'Alienation' is an important concept to which we shall return (see Ch. 6).

The engineering of consent

By the same token as it informs people that they are really things, modern psychology also enables some people, scientists and those with power, to treat the rest as though they were things. They are enabled to do this because of the immediate assumption we make of an absolute right to control the physical world; if people are cast as part of that world, we assume the same right of control over them too.

Not many defenders of positivism are explicit about their ideologies. Fortunately there is at least one exception, in the person of the eminent behavioural scientist, H. J. Eysenck. In an article entitled 'The Technology of Consent,' Eysenck (1969) says:

The problem to be discussed is: how can we engineer a

social consent which will make people behave in a socially adapted, law-abiding fashion, which will not lead to a breakdown of the intricately interwoven fabric of social life? Clearly we are failing to do this: the ever-increasing number of unofficial strikes, the ever-increasing statistics of crime of all sorts, the general alienation on which so many writers have commented are voluble witnesses to this statement. The psychologists would answer that what was clearly required was a technology of consent – that is, a generally applicable method of inculcating suitable habits of socialized conduct into the citizens (and especially the future citizens) of the country in question – or preferably the whole world.

It is hardly necessary to point out the main fallacy in Eysenck's argument. Consent has to be 'engineered' only when it is not given voluntarily. Eysenck's positivism prevents him from seeing social issues in terms of a consent voluntarily given or withheld. It also prevents him from realizing that the problems he speaks of are examples of a *meaningful* dissent from the prevailing order; thus, he cannot bring himself even to consider the underlying reasons for dissent in the unequal distribution of wealth, power, opportunity, and quality of life. He accepts this inequality as given and then delegates to psychology the task of engineering a consent to it. Eysenck does not wish to provide real solutions to the problems he mentions because that would clearly require a major change in the structure of society. Instead he is pleased to sweep these problems under the carpet of a 'consent' which he and his friends are only too anxious to engineer. Few clearer illustrations of ideological tendency in modern psychology could be provided than the short quotation above.

The worship of normality
I said previously that an important characteristic of positivism was its acceptance of present society and the human behaviour essential to it as the only possible social reality. The ideological content here is easily seen; positivism assumes that what men and women are now is what they have always been in the past and always will be. It thus has the effect of discouraging us from thinking about *what man could be*, from exploring man's potential and his ability to live differently in a different social

framework.

The best concrete example of this tendency in psychology is the way in which it worships the statistical norm, especially in the traditional area of personality theory and testing (see D3). The language of normal–abnormal as used in psychology carries with it the unexamined assumption that what is normal in our society is necessarily a good thing. Thus, by a subtle sleight of hand, what is really a value-judgement of immense significance is slipped into psychology's view of man, disguised as a statement of objective fact. For, when we say that some-one is abnormal on some psychological scale or other, we im-mediately think of the personality feature in question as something undesirable that should be corrected. In this way, psychology merely adds to, and gives scientific credence for, the massive pressures society brings to bear on the individual, from birth to death, to conform and be like everybody else, to be respectable and not stray from the path. The argument here is not that conformity to any given society is necessarily bad, but that the merits of conformity to the particular society we find ourselves in should be debated at the very outset of a psychology of human personality. Whether or not one regards normality in our society as the limited, impoverished and de-structive condition so many thinkers are now saying it is, this is at least an evaluation the student of psychology should be required to consider. One of the contributions of R. D. Laing, as we shall see in the next chapter, is to have popularized the notion that our kind of society systematically 'drives people out of their minds'; to be normal in our society is to be a mere shell of obedient conformity with social roles imposed by the culture, at the expense of any contact with the real basis of one's own and others' experience. This opens up a possibility which is inconceivable under positivism's ahistorical view of man – a serious study of *the pathology of normalcy*.

The chief way in which psychology buttresses its perspec-tive of abnormality as undesirable is by an appeal to biolog-ical constructs such as adaptive–maladaptive. Here again we see the fallacy of regarding psychology as nothing more than a special type of biological science, and of viewing man by simple analogy with lower forms of life. If an animal fails to adjust to its environment, we can quite reasonably regard this as undesirable because it would result in an impairment to the

48

animal's chances of survival. But there is an all-important difference between the concept of environment as applied to lower forms of life and as applied to man. The environment of an animal species remains constant or, at least, is not altered by the activity of that species upon it. Man however *makes his own environment* and it is constantly changing as a result of his efforts. Therefore, in the case of man, we cannot simply say that adjustment to his environment is always to be desired, simply because it may be the case that the environment he has created is bad for him and should be radically changed – the historical perspective again.

Let me reinforce the point with a forceful metaphor. The reader is asked to imagine a Nazi concentration camp and to consider two guards who work at the camp. One of these guards is perfectly happy at his job, seems to have few cares or worries, mixes well with the other guards, and so on. The other guard shows all the signs of extreme emotional disturbance, his behaviour is odd, and he does not get along with his fellows. Which of these two guards is normal and which abnormal in anything other than a purely statistical sense? Whose behaviour is adaptive and whose maladaptive in the larger context of human progress? Which one is healthy and which sick? In case the reader thinks this example somewhat exaggerated for our purposes, let me remind her that we are now in a situation where people accept without demur the presence of inhuman, monotonous work, degrading poverty and powerlessness, mechanical and meaningless personal relationships and widespread institutionalized violence in our own society, while every night on their televisions they see evidence of worldwide exploitation, famine, and slaughter without attempting, if they are 'normal' and 'well-adjusted', to do anything about it or even letting it upset them.

The denigration of deviance
The ideological import here is essentially the obverse of that above, but because it contains a few additional implications, I have included it as a separate point. Clearly, the attractions of 'normality' become that much greater if the contrasts in statistically abnormal forms of behaviour are always seen pejoratively. Psychology reinforces its worship of normality by approaching any behaviour which deviates from those

49

norms as, by definition, a reflection of individual maladjustment, emotional immaturity, mental pathology, or some other negatively valued concept. Again, it must be stressed that what is being claimed here is not that social deviance is good as such, but that psychology merely accepts what it takes to be the consensus evaluations of behaviour and incorporates them into its language without acknowledgement. Once more, what is really a moral condemnation of people who are different is made to masquerade as a statement of objective, scientific fact. Young (1971) provides an excellent account of this process, with several revealing examples, in the field of drug-taking – an area in which the irrationalisms and distortions of the positivist view are especially obvious.

We may already guess from the preceding discussion that by stripping the deviant act of its social meaning, by presenting it as mechanistically or in some other way determined, it is immediately denied that the act could possibly be justified from the standpoint of an alternative view of social morality. Whatever its merits may or may not be, the hedonistic, non-competitive worldview of the cannabis user is simply dismissed as the product of emotional immaturity, weak ego-strength, disturbed family background, or some other neurosis-producing agency (see Young, 1971). This example is useful for our purposes because it is easily grasped how the values being denied here are a direct threat to the middle-class values of hard work, self-denial, and economic competition, which are themselves essential to the preservation of the kind of society we have. And the same is true in a less obvious way of many other forms of deviant behaviour.

What then are the added implications of psychology's treatment of deviance? In the first place, by constantly reasserting the meaninglessness of deviant phenomena, psychology helps foster the illusion of a consensus in society. No sane, normal individual, it is implied, could possibly behave in this pathological, abnormal way; everybody is agreed as to what is normal, well-adjusted and socially useful behaviour and those who are not agreed are not responsible for their views, because there must be something wrong with them. The truth is, of course, that society is composed of a variety of social groups with different and often conflicting norms, and that there is a constant battle between these groups to have their own version of reality accepted as the correct one. The group which succeeds will obviously be the group with the most power, in the form of access to the media, access to the legislature and influential support from the 'experts' who give to this particular set of values the gloss of scientific authority. Consequently, what are really the norms of one social group – those with established power and a vested interest in resisting social change – are declared to be the norms of society as a whole.

There is a further advantage to the establishment in psychology's treatment of the deviant, and although it is strictly more relevant to the next chapter, it must be included here for a full account of ideology in psychology. The means by which deviant behaviour is discredited is often by attaching to it some kind of derogatory labels – neurotic, psychotic, psychopathic, and so on. The usefulness of this labelling process is that once you have named something in this way, as a recognizable entity in need of 'treatment', 'modification', or some other form of correction, you are thereby enabled to control it and remove whatever threat the behaviour poses to the orderly continuation of your world. Thus, psychology and especially psychiatry have very practical benefits to offer the establishment. Moreover, this correction and control is all the while presented as a humane and enlightened posture towards the unfortunate, thereby disguising its true significance in the battle of opposing moral and political positions.

Maddison (1973) has shown the workings of this strategy by describing the role of the psychiatrist in labelling student militants as mentally ill.

Individualization
The final point in this list of ideological tendencies concentrates on one particular inadequacy of positivistic psychology: namely, its preferences for viewing human beings as isolated individuals, abstracted from the world of social and economic forces which bear upon their lives. When this inherent bias in psychology's approach is applied to practical human affairs, the result is that *phenomena more usefully seen as social problems are dismissed as evidence of individual maladjustment.*

Apart from the notion of mental illness, which I will be dealing with shortly, the chief culprit here is the concept of 'personality'. As used by psychologists this concept almost always implies that behaviour is caused by something *inside* the person – some inner dynamic formed in early childhood: some 'trait' she has mysteriously acquired: some 'conditioned response' she has picked up probably, as George Kelly somewhere has it, when she wasn't looking. Moreover, these internal causes of behaviour invariably originate in the past; either the person was born with them or has learned to behave in that way, usually a long time ago. What all this ignores, of course, is that we live in a complex system of social and economic forces which constrain our behaviour by setting limits – in the form of laws, informal expectations or, more simply, sheer economic necessity – on what it is possible for us to do. It also ignores the fact that people are capable of representing the world to themselves, however imperfectly, and acting on that basis, and that an explanation of behaviour may often be found in someone's *present* circumstances without recourse to past events. Finally, it ignores the possibility that people may protest against their social circumstances, however inarticulately, unsuccessfully, and with consequent suffering to themselves and others.

One of the clearest illustrations of these particular distortions is to be found in the area of crime. The great majority of recorded crime is committed by a single section of society – the lower working class or 'disreputable poor'. Equally, most crimes are crimes against property. So, these two elementary facts about crime add up to the statement that a great deal of it consists of the theft of other peoples' property by the poorest, least privileged members of the community. Surely here is an unavoidable invitation to at least include in our explanation of crime the unequal distribution of wealth in society, if not to begin with that fact. But no! The leading British theory is that crime is the result of a special type of personality, caused by the activity of some mysterious part of the brain (Eysenck, 1970). Thus a psychology which purports to explain crime makes no mention whatever of the brutalizing effects of crowded, insanitary living conditions, appalling educational facilities, severely limited work and recreational opportunities, periodic unemployment, and almost total lack of power to improve the quality of life. And no mention also of the possibility that the future delinquent may appreciate his position at the bottom of society's heap, become justifiably

52

bitter about it and conclude that he has nothing to lose by a life of crime. The reader will understand by now why it is that these things are unmentionable in psychology and disappear behind the smokescreen of individualistic explanations. To mention them might suggest to too many people that something should be done to change them, and what might become of the psychologist's comfortable way of life then?

The 'expert' as definer of reality

In the last section I presented a list of ways in which psychology could be regarded as ideological. I now intend to look at the same material from a different perspective and divide it in a way which cuts across the substantive areas of ideology we have been examining. This new division corresponds roughly with what is meant by the 'pure' and the 'applied' branches of psychology and to the theory as opposed to the practice of the subject. In terms of ideology itself, it distinguishes between the way psychology is used to influence men's minds and, on a much more concrete level, to exercise direct control over their lives. I will deal with the 'pure', ideational aspect first.

It is now a commonplace in sociological thinking that reality is socially constructed; that is to say, our knowledge of the world, including our knowledge of ourselves and our institutions, is something which is *created* by human beings in interaction with each other and must therefore be itself understood as a social process. What I have suggested several times previously, and now wish to underline, is that not everybody plays an equal part in this process of knowledge-construction; some people's activity is far more important in determining the dominant conceptions man has of himself and his world. These people are, of course, the accredited, generally recognized 'experts', and it is their role in moulding man's self-image that I now want to discuss (see F7).

Not all scientific experts are necessarily charlatans. For example, the chemist has specially acquired knowledge and complex techniques of investigation not available to the rest of us, which enable him quite properly to be an arbiter of our understanding of particular facets of the physical world. But I

53

have already spent some time in this book explaining how this simple model of expertise cannot be transferred to psychology. The psychologist has no special techniques of investigation but only pretends to have. And the knowledge the psychologist has acquired of human behaviour is of a narrow, trivial kind which, as we have seen, ruthlessly distorts our natural experience of life. There may be senses in which it is possible for one person to know more of human behaviour and experience than another, but positivistic knowledge is not one of them.

Each age in human history has had a characteristic self-image, a description of human nature which reflected the stage of historical development in which it occurred. Previously these self-images were conveyed by myth and by religion but now, in accordance with our particular stage of development with its worship of technology, they are the product of science and scientists. Let us recall the areas of ideology given above and rehearse our understanding of how the image of man presented in these examples fits in with the needs of our present society and is aimed at conserving it.

Laing (1967) insistently points out that in this century men have killed over one hundred million of their fellow men. These have been 'normal' human beings killing other 'normal' human beings. The conclusion from this single observation is that to be normal in our age is to be, in the most meaningful sense of the word, insane. It is no accident that the image of man offered by modern psychology is also insane. Can the reader make the leap of imagination required to realize this? A psychology which ignores the fact of human experience, rejects that experience as having no connection with behaviour and pretends that the mere manipulation of behaviour *is* the study of man, *that psychology is mad*: it denies what we all know is there, and then denies that it has denied it. Patients in mental hospital who claim that they or others are machines are labelled insane by psychiatrists. What then of the scientific experts who say exactly the same thing?

But there is method in this madness. Our society *requires* that people think of themselves as machines or mere organisms. It crucially depends on people being cut off from their experience, because if they once listened to their experience, to their yearnings for creativity, genuine love, fulfilment, they might cease to be the automata the machine demands. The technological machine insists on an attenuation of human possibilities, on a bleak uniformity of taste, and a curtailment of aspirations in its producers and consumers, for only thus can it continue to churn out its redundant wares. The psychology of our age, then, must see men as objects, or as behaviour-emitting organisms, because that is what the system requires them to be. Again, it is no accident that behaviourism arose at about the same time and in the same place as the most advanced capitalist system the world has known, and shortly after the invention by Henry Ford of the production line. The rat in the Skinner box, mindlessly and monotonously working and consuming in its barren, 'structured' environment is a parody of modern man's situation in advanced capitalism – Henry Ford's dream. We have a dehumanizing psychology in a dehumanized society. T. S. Eliot was right: we *are* the hollow men and we have a hollow psychology to prove it.

Not only does our society require a split between people's experience and their behaviour, but also a split between the individual and the society she lives in, and this too is reflected in our psychology. Men *can* make their own history, create their own environments and sometimes do, but it is essential to the continuation of the machine that most of them do not realize this. Qualitative changes in society occur when large numbers of human beings suddenly understand that *society is not a thing*, which exists independently of them, which has always been there in its present form and to which they must adjust themselves, but is instead *a man-made creation* for which they are, or could be, responsible. That is why, as part of the attempt to prevent them from understanding this, there exists the split between the academic disciplines of psychology and sociology, where one studies the individual as a thing and the other studies society as a thing and ne'er the twain shall meet. That is also why modern psychology depicts man as isolated from the context of the man-made world he lives in. To put him back into that world immediately invites the dangerous thought that poverty, degradation, and oppression are not just 'there', but are men's responsibility and can be changed.

In the last few paragraphs we have been looking at aspects of the concept of alienation and we have by no means finished with this concept. Let me conclude this section, however, by stating that *positivistic psychology is an alienated and alienating psychology and that is why it is ideological.*

The question of control

We now turn to the other side of the coin, to the way in which psychology is employed to justify the direct control of human lives. As I have already said, this kind of ideological function may be discovered in psychology's so-called applied fields – clinical, educational, criminal, and industrial – although the most outstanding example of ideological social control is psychiatry. However, I shall be devoting the next chapter to psychiatry and will therefore omit discussion of it here.

Psychology is used in diverse ways to control lives. There is, for example, the practice of psychological testing in which alleged psychological characteristics are measured to enable people to be classified and disposed of in various ways. Again, I would prefer to leave a discussion of this until later and concentrate here on one particular brand of behaviourism in practice, the ironically titled 'radical behaviourism' of B. F. Skinner and the operant technology of behaviour modification that goes with it (see A3).

There are two reasons for this emphasis. First, Skinner is probably the most influential psychologist alive today and his growing band of followers are the strongest, best-organized, single group of psychologists in the applied fields. In addition, unlike most psychologists, Skinner has been quite explicit about the political implications of his work, and has described a utopian vision of a future society founded on his principles (see B1). And Skinner's (1972) latest book, *Beyond Freedom and Dignity*, has raised a storm of controversy. He is thus the true inheritor in psychology of Comte's grandiose plans for a 'scientific' society. All this has rubbed off on his disciples, whose enthusiasm for their work often reaches the level of apostolic fervour. Skinnerian ideas and methods have invaded all branches of applied psychology, and are applicable in principle to any area of human affairs where the control of human behaviour is deemed to be desirable.

The second reason for concentrating on Skinner is that behaviour modification principles represent a model of what all other positivistic psychologies attempt to do. In an important sense, the Skinnerian position is the most intelligent brand of behaviourism because it cuts through the mystification and confusion and is brutally frank about what applied behaviour theory really is – *a technology for getting people to do what you want them to do.*

I will assume that the reader is familiar with the main concepts and principles of behaviour modification (see A3). The basic idea behind the technology is that 'behaviour is shaped and maintained by its consequences'. The job of the behaviour modifier is simply to arrange these consequences, that is, to structure the organism's environment, so that suitable, desirable behaviour is emitted. Now, it is these words 'suitable' and 'desirable' which immediately raise a moral and political question. Who decides what is desirable behaviour and what is not? In practice, of course, it is the psychologist who decides. Usually the justification for the decision is taken to be self-evident; there is little or no discussion. But when pushed Skinnerians will usually admit that their definitions of desirable behaviour are taken from the norms of the *present* society, that 'desirable' means normal, conventional, and respectable. In other words, what is desirable is what conforms to their own limited, middle-class values. Perhaps the reader can now see what I mean by the frank quality of the Skinnerian system. It is frankly a technology for normalizing people's behaviour. The experience accompanying that behaviour, the emotions perhaps of grief, despair, rage or joy, the meaning of the behaviour in terms of the person's experience of life, all this is dismissed as irrelevant – mere epiphenomena with no bearing on behaviour and no place in a scientific discourse. All that is considered is overt behaviour and whether or not it conforms to the psychologist's authoritarian standards. Skinnerian psychology is the essence of insane psychology in practice.

And then there is the question of power. No behaviour modification programme can work unless the psychologist has a monopoly on the things his charges want, the 're-inforcers'. Take a Token Economy System (see A3, F2) in which a mental hospital ward, say, is organized by making the provision of tokens, which can then be used to buy goods, contingent upon the occurrence of specified, desirable behaviours

57

in the patients. A reinforcer commonly used is cigarettes. I have known treatment programmes for cigarette-smoking patients to crumble because kindly relatives brought in cigarettes for the patients during visiting hours. The programme crumbled, obviously, because the patient no longer had to do what she was told in order to get cigarettes. Such programmes can only work when the person to be modified is powerless in terms of access to the things she wants, and it is the powerless of society – chronic psychiatric patients, imprisoned criminals, and the intellectually retarded – who form the involuntary clients for behaviour modification programmes.

To complicate the issue, I will admit that Token Economy Systems are generally preferable to allowing chronic psychiatric patients to rot away neglected in mental hospitals. I would also agree that what are called behaviour modification schemes for these patients, and for the intellectually retarded, can sometimes be justified as educational programmes, provided their *explicit* aim is to give the individual more control over her destiny, not less. However, we do not need the dehumanized jargon of the Skinnerians to explain the efficacy of genuine praise and encouragement; it could also be the case that beneficial effects occur because for once the patients are being noticed and recognized as human beings with needs and aspirations. But, if so, this is a far cry from operant technology, and the committed Skinnerian would never concede the possibility of what has just been said, since the terms 'freedom' and 'dignity' are meaningless for him.

It is when it is applied to areas like delinquency that the totalitarian, '1984' aspects of Skinner's psychology become more obvious. The behaviour modifiers would claim here that delinquent behaviour is clearly undesirable and that there can be no dispute that they are justified in attempting to suppress it. But is this really so obvious? Take the situation of a large American city like Detroit and assume also a time of race riots, as in the recent past, in which most of the delinquents arrested are looting stores in the centre of the city owned by rich white men. Now the line here between delinquent behaviour and political protest is very thin indeed, if it can be drawn at all. To my mind, the suppression of delinquent behaviour in this case, by behaviour modification or any other means, is a political act and should be seen as such. The danger of the scientistic approach to such social problems is that their political content is thereby hidden behind a technical and supposedly value-free methodology, which is, indeed, precisely its attraction. I will return to this point when we come to discuss the applied areas of psychology in more detail, but I want to make clear that I have chosen the area of crime here because it illustrates most clearly the authoritarian potential of behaviour modification. The same arguments about change versus stasis in society apply to any field of behaviour.

What is the purpose of a science of psychology?

By way of summarizing this chapter, let us remind ourselves of the positivistic definition of psychology – the prediction and control of behaviour (and, sometimes, of experience). We have seen that, first of all, this definition is predicated on the notion that it is possible to have a human science which is value-free in the same sense that the physical sciences are thought to be value-free. However, we have also seen that this is an impossibility, and that values lie at the very core of the human sciences. The prediction and control of some people by some others *cannot* be free of values.

We have attempted in this chapter to answer the question why it is that psychology is presented as value-free when it so obviously is not. It is because by this means a certain set of hidden, and for the most part unconscious, values are allowed full scope, without the embarrassment of public scrutiny or debate. These values are ideological in that they focus on a specific purpose – the conservation of the status quo in society. Although this ideology is manifest in several particular ways, it has two aspects, corresponding to its mythic and its concrete functions: namely, the 'expert' definition of human and social reality and the direct control of lives.

The reader may ask at this point what the alternative is to this state of affairs. Does it make a scientific psychology impossible? The answer, as in the last chapter, is no! What we have to do, though, is to make our values regarding human nature and society quite explicit, make them available for open discussion, and *then* proceed to gather the knowledge required to develop human potential in the chosen direction. It is in this sense that psychology becomes *a moral science* (see F7).

What kind of knowledge will this be, since it will clearly not be positivistic knowledge? It would be far too ambitious to attempt a definitive answer to this question here. All that can be said is that psychology should seek the task of developing forms of inquiry by means of which people might arrive at a greater understanding of, and a greater degree of control over, *their own* behaviour and experience, *their own* relationships with others, and *their own* place in the social order. Thus, psychology would cease to be a commodity marketable to those with power and a vested interest in things as they are, and would become a truly *democratic* undertaking of potential benefit to all.

4
Psychiatry and anti-psychiatry

In Chapter 2 I said that most radical criticism in psychology has been directed at behaviourism and psychiatry and it is now time to consider the second of these targets. In the last chapter I mentioned that psychiatry was the outstanding example of ideological psychology in practice, that it was designed for the concrete control of people in the service of our technological/consumer society, and it is now time to substantiate this claim. Once again, the justification for this control is a form of positivism.

The positivism espoused by psychiatry is of a different kind from that found in academic psychology in that it does not extend the positivistic perspective to all human beings but only to those it declares to be 'mentally ill' (see F1). Conventional psychiatry has no general theory of human functioning but implicitly assumes that 'normal' people are, in some vague way, rational creatures responsible for their choices, etc. This responsibility it withdraws from psychiatric patients, believing that their experience and behaviour are determined by some disease-process acting upon them and are therefore out of their control. These diseases, like other diseases, are things which *happen* to people, independently of their volition; the person to whom the disease happens has nothing to do with the matter. Thus, in psychiatry, man is dehumanized by being transformed into a thing or a biological system as a consequence of 'mental illness'. The positivistic effort in psychiatry is the attempt *to force the practical management of human conduct into the realm of the medical sciences.*

It might be as well to insert a few words here regarding the relationship between Freudian psychology (see D3) and positivism. Although the great majority of psychiatrists practising in this country would reject psychoanalysis, it is still a significant part of the modern psychiatric scene and most hospitals will have at least one analyst on their staff. Freudian psychology *does* constitute a theory of normal functioning and this is, indeed, a positivistic theory, in the sense that it denies human responsibility and choice and is alleged to be strictly objective and value-free. Adolescent and adult behaviour is regarded as being fixed by the vicissitudes of the child's first five years of life in interaction with its parents. More fundamentally, behaviour is said to be determined by the fate of biological instincts of which the conscious individual is unaware. Thus, the main burden of psychoanalysis is positivistic and it was Freud who put the weight of his authority behind the concept of 'psychic determinism'. However, the great paradox of psychoanalysis is that the treatment method Freud devised, as distinct from the theory it was supposed to be based on, can easily be seen as an exercise in liberation from determining forces. Although Freud's early dream was to reduce experience and behaviour to neurology and although as a medical doctor he thought in terms of illness and 'psychopathology', he described the aim of his treatment by saying 'where id was there shall ego be', suggesting that after analysis the patient was more in control of her destiny than she was before. The degree and kind of positivism in psychoanalysis no doubt depends on whose hands the theory is in and how the massive body of Freud's thought is interpreted. This is a complex question we shall not be able to resolve here but we shall return to psychoanalysis later in the book.

These qualifications hardly affect the main line of our argument since all psychiatry, whether psychoanalytic or not, claims to be part of medical science. The reader, like anyone else in our culture, will have been bombarded with propaganda from government and other agencies to the effect that 'mental illness is an illness just like any other'. Psychiatry's claim to be an orthodox part of medical science thus rests on the crucial

62

concept of mental illness, but we shall discover this concept to be an absurdity.

The non-concept of mental illness

I should not really have used the term 'non-concept'. A concept is a concept, something we use to classify the events with which we are confronted so that we can deal with them. There is no way in which one can deny the existence of a concept; one can only ask whether it is meaningful and useful. I shall argue that the concept of mental illness is misleading, meaningless, and dangerous, and that is why I have called it a non-concept.

It is essential for the reader to understand that for the vast majority of its practitioners psychiatry is regarded as simply another medical speciality. Whereas, say, paediatrics is the medical speciality dealing with diseases of children and dermatology is devoted to diseases of the skin, psychiatry is taken to be that branch of medicine dealing with diseases of the mind, no different in principle from the rest. Qualified psychiatrists have all gone through a lengthy and complete medical education and have then acquired a smattering of psychology as postgraduates. This shows the priorities the profession holds to. However, owing chiefly to the early influence of psychoanalysis, looked upon with horror and revulsion by the stuffy medical fraternity, psychiatry has long been regarded within medicine as the most disreputable and least prestigious branch. This is very embarrassing for psychiatrists and a great deal of their activity, particularly the insistence · on · meaningless diagnoses and crude, physical methods of treatment, is motivated by a desire to be seen as respectable doctors. In the same way that academic psychologists hunger for the respectability of the physical sciences, psychiatrists yearn for the security of legitimate medicine. Unfortunately for them their efforts are doomed to eventual failure because *psychiatry is not another medical speciality but a quasi-medical illusion.*

If it *is* a legitimate part of medicine we should expect psychiatry to be similar in operation to other medical specialities and psychiatrists to conduct their business similarly to other doctors. We shall see, however, that it is not and they do not.

The unreliability of psychiatric diagnosis

The most obvious sense in which psychiatry is made to resemble general medicine is in the use of the diagnostic system for classifying its patients. Classification in psychiatry, as in legitimate medicine, consists of a collection of discrete, logically mutually exclusive 'disease entities', which are assumed to designate some underlying disease process or cause of the illness, the observable signs and symptoms resulting from this process, and, hopefully, the method of treatment indicated to eliminate the underlying cause and banish the symptoms (see F3).

It is worth noting at the outset that at least two of the logical requirements of a diagnostic system are not met by psychiatry. The categories used are *not* mutually exclusive; there is considerable overlap between them. A patient presenting with a specific set of 'symptoms' may be classified in one of several ways. For example, someone who is anxious and depressed may be diagnosed either as 'anxiety state with depressive features' or as 'neurotic depression with anxiety features', depending on the whim of the diagnostician. Moreover, the important diagnosis of schizophrenia is a disjunctive category, which means that patients may be included in it who have no symptoms whatever in common.

It is not surprising given this state of affairs that psychiatric diagnoses have been shown to be extremely unreliable. This unreliability may be demonstrated in two ways. First, different psychiatrists use the same diagnostic categories with entirely different relative frequencies. One may have a penchant for diagnosing schizophrenia, while another rarely uses this diagnosis and calls everybody depressed. The use of the system is extremely arbitrary. Not only are there large differences between psychiatrists working alongside each other, but there are also huge, general differences between geographical areas. It is well known that schizophrenia is diagnosed much more often in the United States than in Britain, where depression is correspondingly more frequently used. Secondly, many studies have shown that the degree of agreement between psychiatrists independently diagnosing the same patients is very low. More-over, this disagreement increases with an increase in the number of psychiatrists making the diagnosis. When this number exceeds six, as few as 10 per cent of patients are given the same diagnosis. This level of disagreement would be entirely unacceptable in any branch of legitimate medicine.

The invalidity of psychiatric diagnosis

The primary purpose of making a diagnosis is to enable a suitable treatment to be decided upon. The aim of the treatment is, if course, to eliminate the underlying cause of the disease where this is known. Unfortunately, in psychiatry very few 'causes' are definitely established. The exceptions are confined to the organic syndromes where specific lesions to the nervous system are recognized. In the so-called functional illnesses, where the organic basis is either unknown or assumed not to exist, there are a multitude of theories and explanations in competition with each other, and which explanation is chosen depends almost entirely on the prejudices of the psychiatrist concerned – not that it makes a great deal of difference in most cases. Such a chaotic state of affairs exists in no other branch of medicine. Again, it is not surprising, in view of the above, that there is only a 50 per cent chance of predicting what treatment a patient will receive on the basis of her diagnosis. Once more, this would be intolerable in legitimate medicine.

Pseudopatients

A most startling demonstration of the arbitrary nature of psychiatric diagnosis has recently been provided by Rosenhan (1973), who showed that, not only do psychiatrists have great difficulty in distinguishing reliably between different classes of so-called mental illness, they cannot even sort out mental illness from 'normality'. In this study, eight sane individuals with no psychiatric history or evidence of abnormal behaviour presented themselves to twelve different psychiatric hospitals in America. They each made the simple, identical complaint that they had been hearing 'voices', of a kind which have no counterpart in the psychiatric literature. Apart from this and a falsification of name and employment, for self-protection, the pseudopatients behaved in their normal manner and answered all questions truthfully; they in no way tried to 'act crazy' or imitate psychiatric patients. All these individuals were admitted to hospital and diagnosed as psychotic, seven being labelled 'schizophrenic' and one 'manic-depressive'. Following admission, the pseudopatients gave up their complaints of hallucinations and tried to behave as normally and cooperatively as possible. Despite stays in hospital ranging from seven to fifty-two days, none of the pseudopatients were detected as such. (To be more accurate none were detected by the staff. The only people to suspect them of not being genuine were other patients!)

The point of this exercise was not simply to show that some psychiatrists are no good at their job; the variety of hospitals sampled included some very prestigious institutions. Rather, the study showed that strict criteria separating sane from insane behaviour do not exist, as would be expected if mental illness were anything like bodily illness. The factors which lead to psychiatric diagnoses being made appear to have very little to do with characteristics of the patients themselves, the alleged symptoms from which they suffer, but have a great deal to do with the environmental context in which the patients are found. The very fact that these pseudopatients presented themselves at psychiatric hospitals meant for the staff that there *must* be something wrong with them and, given that expectation, their behaviour was 'pathologized' to conform with it. Once one has the notion firmly planted in the mind, it becomes possible to see virtually *any* behaviour as symptomatic of 'mental illness'.

This experiment had an astonishing sequel. In order to check that psychiatrists were not merely erring on the side of caution, Rosenhan informed a teaching and research hospital, which is reckoned to be the best, of his previous results and told the staff to expect some more pseudopatients over the following three months. In fact, none were sent. It subsequently emerged that out of 193 genuine patients admitted for treatment during this period, no less than 41 were alleged with a high degree of confidence to be pseudopatients by at least one member of staff. This finding speaks for itself.

Cultural relativity

So far in this section we have been examining the, as it were, surface characteristics of psychiatry and we have seen how its diagnostic system lacks the objectivity, reliability, and precision required of a legitimate medical speciality. This does not in itself prove that psychiatry's claim is spurious; it just makes it very likely that it is. But there are other, more satisfactory ways of showing that psychiatry is distinct from general medicine.

Anthropologists are constantly reminding us that 'normal' and 'abnormal' are culturally relative terms; what is unquestioningly seen as normal in one culture may be regarded as definitely abnormal in another. Although this fact is often admitted by psychiatrists, its obvious implications are rarely taken to heart. Any conception of illness or disease must be defined in contrast to some norm of ideal functioning. In general medicine this norm may be objectively and universally defined, in principle, in terms of the healthy physiological functioning of the human body. This does, of course, entail the value-judgement that such healthy functioning is a good thing, but this value-judgement, like the ultimate aim of the physical sciences, is hardly contentious. But in psychiatry, dealing as it does with social behaviour, no such objective and universal norm may be described, since the definition of 'normal' varies from culture to culture and from one historical epoch to another. Presumably, bronchitis is the same wherever and whenever in the world it occurs, but what is denigrated as 'schizophrenia' in our culture may be highly prized as evidence of some mystical power in another. And the reader has probably heard it remarked that if Christ were alive today and began turning over the tables of the 'money-lenders', his feet would hardly touch the ground on the way to the nearest mental hospital. So, the criteria psychiatry uses in judging what is abnormal behaviour are taken from the prevailing norms of the times we live in and must therefore be seen in a moral context and not a medical context. I shall have more to say about the consequences of this simple observation later in the chapter but let us rest content here with the conclusion that *the fact of cultural relativity makes psychiatry an entirely different kind of enterprise from legitimate medicine.*

Szasz's argument

The crux of psychiatry's claim to be part of legitimate medicine is, as we have seen, the validity of the concept 'mental illness', and therefore the most satisfactory method of rejecting this claim is a logical argument showing this concept to be either meaningless or misleading. Although the lines of this argument are well known to those with objections to psychiatry, it has been most cogently stated by Szasz (1960).

The argument is essentially very simple. There are two senses in which the concept of mental illness has been used by psychiatrists. First, the 'organicist' position is that mental illnesses result from diseases of the brain and nervous system, which diseases then affect the mind and behaviour. In this case, it would be better to call these illnesses 'diseases of the brain', since that is what they are. To persist in calling them mental illnesses is misleading because it confuses the neurological defect, which must be seen in an anatomical and physiological context, with whatever 'problems in living' the patient has, which must be seen in an ethical and social context. For example, epilepsy is a symptom of brain damage, and from a medical point of view must be understood within the framework of neurology. However, the 'problems in living' (Szasz's term) the epileptic may encounter – the stigma of the illness, the hostility of the ignorant and superstitious, the difficulty in finding suitable work – these are not themselves medical problems but social and ethical problems. The term 'mental illness' serves to obfuscate the distinction between two entirely different kinds of problem and should be abandoned. The reason it is not abandoned by the organicists is that these psychiatrists would be doing themselves out of a job, because psychiatry would then become a part of neurology which is, of course, the medical speciality which deals with diseases of the brain. Moreover, only a small part of the caseload of psychiatry is of this kind, where the neurological basis of the disease is understood. Although the organicists would also lay claim to the huge areas of schizophrenia and psychotic depression, they have no evidence for a neurological substrate in these instances, only a presumption. And there remain large areas of psychiatry, the neuroses and 'personality disorders', which the organicists would admit were not bodily diseases in any sense. To sum up then, if by 'mental illness' one means diseases of the brain, it would be far better to call them that and for this part of psychiatry to become a branch of neurology.

The other sense in which 'mental illness' is used is quite different from the above. In this use, it is conceded that there is no physiological disturbance, no illness of the body, but there is nevertheless alleged to be some illness of the 'mind' or 'personality'. Now, what can this mean? In what sense may we think of the mind as being diseased? Clearly, we are dealing here with *a metaphor*, a concept originating in the organic universe of discourse and transferred to the area of experience and social behaviour. We have an analogous use of the same metaphor in the phrase 'a sick society'. But of what use is this metaphor? What does it tell us? Nothing, for the logic of its use is *circular*, comprising both a description and a cause. In the complex world we live in, many people are unable to cope with the demands society makes upon them, the behaviour of many others simply does not fit in with the needs of this society, and nearly all of us, at some time or another, experience unhappiness as a consequence of complicated personal relationships. These are the behaviours and experiences which are designated, metaphorically, as 'mental illnesses' and this is merely an abstraction to provide a descriptive cover for the phenomena in question. However, the same abstraction is then employed as a putative *cause* of the said behaviours and experiences. Here is the circularity. What is mental illness? Certain kinds of experiences and behaviours. What causes these experiences and behaviours? Mental illness. And so on. Thus, an analysis of the concept of mental illness in this second sense leaves it floating, as it were, in mid-air, attached to nothing, telling us nothing, devoid of meaning. Its main effect on our thought is to mislead us into thinking of intentional, meaningful action, properly regarded in the context of human values, as involuntary behaviour caused by some entirely abstract 'illness' and therefore part of a spuriously objective branch of medical science. Szasz (1970) has devoted an entire book to a comparison between the concept of mental illness and that of witchcraft, which preceded it in the 'explanation' of abnormal behaviour. Szasz does not merely suggest that they are similar concepts but that they reflect a single phenomenon, serving the same political purpose, masquerading in different forms at different times. We shall see why he argues this when we come to consider more of Szasz's work later on.

What is being denied?

Before ending this section, I should like to clear up some possible misunderstandings that often arise when one attacks the concept of mental illness. First of all, it is not being denied that many people treated by psychiatry experience emotional suffering, often extreme, for which they deserve compassion and, if they ask for it, help. But emotional suffering or un-happiness is *not* illness, it is emotional suffering or unhappiness. Secondly, it is not being denied that some people's behaviour is bizarre or unusual. But deviant behaviour does *not* necessarily betoken illness, except when it can be shown that it is primarily the result of some neurological lesion. Even then, the deviance is not some quality inherent in the illness itself, but depends on some moral evaluation of the behaviour in question, made by the person herself or, more often, by others. This leads us conveniently to a consideration of a sociological contribution to the understanding of so-called mental illness.

Rule-breaking, labelling, and deviance

The reader may well be asking this question: if the phenomena dealt with by psychiatry are not illnesses, what are they? One answer which has been proposed by sociologists is that they are examples of a particular kind of deviant behaviour.

Deviancy theory is that branch of sociology concerned with rule-breaking behaviour (that is, with behaviour which clearly transgresses agreed-on social norms), with the sanctions imposed on rule-breakers by society as a consequence of these transgressions, and with the effect of these sanctions on the rule-breaker's subsequent identity and career in life. Scheff (1966) has posited that the kind of rules which are broken by those called mentally ill are *residual rules*. Scheff defines these rules as the *unnamable* expectations we have of such things as 'decency' and 'reality'.

Thus, by residual rule-breaking Scheff refers to behaviours

which, because they violate inarticulate, taken-for-granted rules, are not easily understandable by most members of society, including psychiatrists, since categories do not exist to account for them. They are, therefore, likely to be found strange and frightening. Scheff's analysis is, perhaps, more directly pertinent, not to mental illness in general, but to the particular class of it called schizophrenia. This huge class, which accounts for roughly one quarter of *all* health service inpatients of any kind in this country, has been regarded by many observers, including some psychiatrists, as a 'rag-bag', into which are put all those whose behaviour is unintelligible from a common-sense point of view.

There is an important difference, however, between rule-breaking and deviance. Becker (1963) explains:

> Social groups create deviance by making the rules whose infraction constitutes deviance, and by applying those rules to particular people and labelling them as outsiders. From this point of view, deviance is not a quality of the act a person commits, but rather a consequence of the application by others of rules and sanctions to an 'offender'. The deviant is one to whom that label has successfully been applied; deviant behaviour is behaviour that people so label.

Becker's distinction between rule-breaking and deviance may become clearer by describing two vital consequences which flow from it. In the case of schizophrenia, we would expect the residual rule-breaking it denotes to arise from fundamentally different sources, and this is precisely what Scheff maintains. The original source of rule-breaking might be organic or psychological, the result of external stress or of deliberate acts of defiance. All these sources would be found included under the label because 'schizophrenia' does not owe its existence to the uniform behaviour of a group of rule-breakers but to the labelling behaviour of others who find this rule-breaking unintelligible. Furthermore, we would also expect that the label would fail to include the great majority of people who have broken residual rules. Behaviour of this kind, says Scheff, is widespread but mostly of transitory significance. It becomes evidence of 'schizophrenia' or some other mental illness only when the transgressor is publicly labelled by psychiatrists as an *official deviant* or, in medical

71

terminology, when a diagnosis is made.

The effect of this labelling process upon how a person regards herself, her identity, has been the subject of much attention by deviancy theorists. As we have seen, most residual rule-breaking is transitory, goes unacknowledged and unrecorded by official agencies and will, therefore, have little effect on identity, because it is rationalized by the person and others in terms different from illness. However, various factors, such as a low tolerance threshold in the relevant community or a low social status on the part of the transgressor, make it likely that some of this rule-breaking will be labelled as mental illness. This sets up a system of mutual expectations between the labellers and those so labelled. Owing to the learning of stereotypes of mental illness in childhood, and to the frequent reinforcement of these stereotypes in the media and, often inadvertently, in ordinary conversation, the *deviant role* of the mental patient – head-case, loony, etc. – already exists in the community's imagery waiting to be filled. (The fact that these stereotypes vary from culture to culture accounts for the diverse and specific forms mental illness takes in different parts of the world.) The labelled person is rewarded for playing this deviant role because it fits with the expectations now held by doctors, patients, relatives, and others. Further, if she attempts to return to a conventional role, she is punished by the effect of *stigma* resulting from these same expectations. Note that Scheff is not suggesting that mental illness is merely a matter of pretence and malingering (as Szasz often appears to believe). It is a question of *identity*, of the constant task self-conscious human beings face of deciding who they are and how they are to conduct themselves. Scheff suggests that in the crisis engendered when a residual rule-breaker is publicly labelled, she is highly confused and suggestible and may therefore accept the role of mental patient offered to her as the only available alternative. We shall see later, in the work of Erving Goffman, how the institution of the psychiatric hospital exerts almost irresistible pressure on its patients to conform to this role.

I have devoted some space to Scheff's *deviancy model* because I wanted to make it clear that there does exist an alternative to the *medical model* for explaining much of what is now called mental illness. The validity of Scheff's particular theoretical position must depend, of course, upon empirical studies in the field, but there is already much evidence to favour his main propositions.

Before leaving this topic, I should emphasize that Scheff's theory cannot be said to apply to *all* psychiatric patients. The deviancy perspective on mental illness in general applies best to those individuals whose behaviour is complained about by others; the paradigm case is, as I said, the diagnosis of schizophrenia. It applies less well to those who are not complained about, but who themselves complain and seek help. This distinction between the complaining and the complained about is one that is intended to be drawn in principle; in practice, the distinction is by no means clear. For one thing, many of those who present themselves to their doctor apparently voluntarily have been persuaded to do so by relatives because their behaviour had become disturbing. However, there are instances, chiefly among the so-called neuroses, where behaviour is in no way disturbing to, or complained about by, others but in which the person simply requests assistance for insupportable problems in living. Even here, it is likely that the imagery of mental illness and the role of patient play a part in the development and course of the problem. In any case, because deviancy theory has a more limited application in these instances, this does not mean that they are illnesses. They are problems in living and it is by no means certain that the psychiatrist is the best equipped to help with them.

The moral nature of psychiatric intervention

The curious thing about psychiatrists is that many of them seem almost to be aware of the moral nature of their work, without being able to say so explicitly to themselves or others. Anyone with first-hand knowledge of the workings of psychiatry will testify to the strong moral undercurrent present in psychiatrists' attitudes towards their patients. In informal conversations between psychiatrists, some patients will be approved of as fighting bravely to overcome their illness, but many will not. These latter will be denigrated in perfectly ordinary, conventional terms – lazy, deceitful, impertinent, and so on and the patient's reprehensible characteristics will not be distinguished from the illness itself. To overhear one of these conversations is an astonishing experience for someone who has been led to believe that psychiatry is objectice and scientific. Even for psychiatrists, it would appear, the distinction between 'madness' and 'badness' is difficult to sustain.

An important aspect of the relationship between psychiatrists and their patients is difference in social class. Most psychiatrists, like most medical doctors, are born into the middle classes, while the remainder quickly acquire the lifestyle and values of the class to which they aspire. As a member of the medical profession and of the professional middle classes generally, the typical psychiatrist is a model of bourgeois rectitude. Against this, the great majority of psychiatric patients are working class. (The classic study of Hollingshead and Redlich (1958) found that, not only did the working-classes provide a disproportionate number of psychiatric patients, but the diagnoses given them were related to social class, 'schizophrenia' being attributed much more often to working-class patients. In addition, the type of treatment a patient received was also related to class; working class patients tended to receive physical treatments like drugs and ECT, while the middle classes were much more likely to get psychotherapy, presumably it is so much easier for psychiatrists to talk to members of their own class.) It is possible, therefore, to be more specific about the values on which psychiatric intervention is based; they are, generally speaking, *middle class values regarding what is decent, reasonable, proper behaviour and experience applied mainly to working class patients.*

It is necessary for the reader to try to imagine what it must be like to live a life in and out of psychiatric hospitals. Particularly if the patient is from the lower working class, with little education, few skills or abilities, and no money, how immensely powerful a figure must the psychiatrist appear? Backed by the near-magical prestige and influence of the medical profession, psychiatrists do, indeed, have very great power to affect the lives of their unfortunate charges. But psychiatry is only one of the 'Welfare' State agencies that rule the patient's life. Seen through the eyes of the patient, her relationship with her psychiatrist must seem very similar to that with the social security official whose code she must satisfy

74

to obtain money, with the local housing officer who decides whether or not she should have a council flat, and with the magistrate who judges her petty offences. They are all part of a monolithic bureaucracy the powerless individual must manipulate as best she can to survive. No wonder patients sometimes deceive their doctors!

The evaluative underpinning of psychiatry is not confined to the informal aspects we have just been considering. Actually, it is clearly apparent in its formal language and theory. Open any psychiatric journal almost at random and you will find degrading, even downright insulting language applied to patients. The terms, 'inadequate personality', 'weak superego', and 'psychopath' are obvious examples. Psychiatrists are often vexed with the problem of deciding what the patient was like before she became ill, whether she had a 'good' or a 'poor' premorbid personality. The criteria by which this is judged read like a litany of middle class values with respect to hard work, regular habits, and respectable family life, etc. The patient's prognosis is considerably worse if she has had a number of jobs, is suspected of having taken drugs, or is 'cohabiting' instead of being properly married. As for a good premorbid personality, I can recall an occasion when the evidence offered for this attribution was that the patient had been an officer in the RAF and was now a company director! Here is an extract from Mayer-Gross, Slater, and Roth (1960), probably the most widely read psychiatric textbook in Britain, which further illustrates these points:

In early phases (of simple schizophrenia), only an unexpected lack of consideration for the closest relatives and friends, or a reckless neglect of social obligations, may be conspicuous. The patient may even preserve a colourless amiability among strangers, but all deeper feeling seems lost. He may hold down an undemanding job, or engage in superficial relations with the opposite sex which come to nothing. He can make no decision and if he is not supported by indulgent relations, he drifts into poverty and lives in the lowest stratum of society as an unemployable idler, tramp, petty criminal or prostitute etc. Many ineffectual, talentless and sterile dilettanti are simple schizophrenics, as also are some of the hangers-on of harmless sects and philosophies, or aiders and abettors of criminal gangs. Gross neglect and ill treatment of children or of elderly relatives may be found due to an insidious simple schizophrenic illness in the culprit. If affective blunting is combined with a lesser degree of apathy the patient may live an antisocial existence for a considerable time.

In the light of passages like the above, one can only react with amazement to psychiatrists' continued insistence that their practice is an objective branch of medicine. The moral tone of much psychiatric writing is evidence for what psychiatrists are at pains to deny, that their patients are responsible agents and not just diseased organisms.

If we reject psychiatric criteria for 'mental health' or optimal human functioning, what alternative is there? There are two solutions. The first is theoretical: we may take a general, culture-free theory of human nature and develop it to describe 'an ideal man' against which we can compare our actual, imperfect forms of being, remembering all the while that the theory begins and ends with values. On the other hand, we may make empirical studies of people whom most of us would regard as creative, loving, self-actualizing, or as having some other desirable characteristic and find out what they are like and how they got that way, so that we can compare the rest of us to them and hypothesize about what we have to do to resemble them. This is an important part of the human potential movement (see Hampden-Turner, 1971). But however successful these attempts are, I would nevertheless submit that the language of 'health' and 'illness' should be avoided and terms like 'development' and 'optimal living' substituted. This is because the organic metaphor of illness can have such disastrous implications for the way we think about human beings and deal with them and it is some of these harmful consequences I now wish to describe.

The harm of 'mental illness'

So far our criticism of 'mental illness' has been devoted to showing that the concept is either misleading, meaningless, or impossible to define non-evaluatively. We will now need to be more positive in our criticism and reveal the concept to be harmful in very practical senses.

Responsibility and meaning

One of the most obvious attributes of an illness is its impersonal nature. Illnesses *happen* to us; we 'catch' them or acquire them in some other way; they have nothing to do with us personally. Moreover, illnesses are *things* which are seen as external to us but which somehow get imposed on us; they do not involve our *selves*. We do not choose to have illnesses, neither do we usually hold ourselves responsible for their arrival or subsequent course. By the same token, there is little we can do ourselves to get rid of illnesses apart, naturally, from cooperating with medical treatment. When we are ill, we hand over part of the responsibility for ourselves, that part concerned with our illness, to the physician, on the understanding that this is the best way of seeking a cure.

All these connotations of 'illness', which are immediately suggested when we think of what it means to be ill, may be perfectly legitimate and necessary in the context of bodily illness. In the field of experience and behaviour covered by psychiatry however, many workers have come to the conclusion that these deeply ingrained associations serve to hamper their efforts at helping with their clients' problems. These helpers are mainly clinical psychologists but a few, mostly younger, psychiatrists would agree with them.

Consider the creation of a new psychiatric patient in the area of so-called neurosis. The reader should remember that we have a situation in which someone with problems in living comes to attend a *hospital*. Owing to the attempt by psychiatry to be accepted as conventional medicine, departments of psychiatry are increasingly being located in general hospitals, so that on the same day that one individual attends a hospital complaining of anxiety, due, say, to her inability to cope with being a housewife and mother, a friend or relative may be attending the same hospital complaining of a pain in her chest. The effect of presenting her problem in this medical context will mean that the psychiatric patient will expect, on arrival at the hospital, to have something done *to* her; the word 'patient' itself implies that one is the passive recipient of manipulations by others and that one's task is simply to wait *patiently* until the experts have completed their technical interventions. These expectations of the new patient will be encouraged by the fact that she will probably receive a physical examination, be required to answer lots of seemingly irrelevant questions (what did your grandfather die of? was your birth a normal delivery?) and be set arbitrary and un-fathomable 'tests' (arranging coloured bricks in patterns, explaining the meaning of proverbs) designed, apparently, to discover the exact nature of her illness. All these initial con-tacts with psychiatry will seem very mysterious to the patient, since their purpose will not be explained to her and she will rarely grasp the point of them. However, seeing herself as in a similar position to her friend with the painful chest, she will not expect anything else; the doctors know best. The patient's passivity in the face of these technical manipulations will be finally reinforced when she receives her treatment, which will indeed be something done *to* her – usually the prescription of drugs whose names she cannot pronounce and whose purpose she only dimly comprehends. In such ways does psychiatry *mystify* the new patient and lead her to hand over responsi-bility for her life to the medical expert. Thereafter, if she is lucky, she will see her doctor for about ten minutes every month or so.

The harmful consequences of the medical approach to problems in living should be obvious to the reader. Those clinical psychologists and others who try to help their clients find real solutions to their problems, rather than merely washing them away temporarily in chemicals, usually reach the conclusion that successful 'therapy' must engage *the active participation* of the client. More often than not, when the smokescreen of diagnosis and symptom has been penetrated, the root of the client's neurotic problems will be found in unhappy personal relationships and/or stressful social circum-stances. No other person can provide a dramatic 'cure' for these problems; there is no 'magic pill' which will make them suddenly disappear. The helper's first task is often to disabuse the client of the false expectations engendered by the medical construction of her problems. If help is effective, it is by help-ing the client to help herself. The medical model of psychiatry works in precisely the opposite direction of reducing the patient to a helpless consumer of a specialized technology, which does nothing to solve her problems but which, like a conjuring trick, merely makes them appear to go away for the time being.

It is true, however, that this situation of helpless lack of responsibility is attractive to many people, particularly those for whom life is an especially uphill struggle. The cardinal feature of Talcott Parsons' classic description of *the sick role* is that it makes legitimate an exemption from normal social responsibilities. It often happens in psychiatry that people become stuck in this way of adapting to life's demands.

Closely related to this surrender of responsibility is a negation of the meaning of the patient's problems in personal and social terms, thus reducing still further the chances of her finding a real solution to them. We have seen that the patient will regard her illness as a thing, isolated from the personally meaningful context of her life. For example, owing to the diffusion of 'mental illness' ideology in the culture, many working class patients will adopt a kind of bodily illness construction of their problems; they complain that there is something wrong with their 'nerves'. It is not *me* that has the problem, these patients are led to say, but my nerves. Psychiatrists do not discourage patients from this manner of thinking because it fits conveniently with, and is hardly less vague than, their own perspective. Although better educated patients may use a more sophisticated vocabulary, they make the same mistake of *reification* – transforming a meaningful process into a meaningless thing. One no longer *is* depressed: one *has* a depression, in the same sense that one *has* a cold. Psychiatrists have recently become excited by the surprising, to them, discovery that 'life-events', such as bereavements, marriages, and changes of job, often precede the onset of psychiatric illness. Even here, though, the relation between the event and the illness is presented in a compartmentalized, mechanical fashion; little or no attempt is made to integrate both life-events and 'illness' in a biographically significant account of the person's experience of life. Thus, psychiatric ideology works, in this respect, as a kind of Medusa's head, turning to stone our understanding of living, personal reality and beguiling us into mistaking meaningful social processes for arbitrary natural occurrences over which we ourselves could never exercise control.

Physical methods of treatment

It is the use of physical methods of treatment which has aroused the most vociferous protests against psychiatry. The employment of such methods, and the justification for describing them as 'treatment' in the first place, is predicated, of course, upon the notion of mental illness. There are three kinds of physical treatment used in modern psychiatry – drugs, ECT, and psychosurgery. I shall comment on each in turn.

The invention and development during the 1950s of the major tranquillizers, such as chlorpromazine and trifluoperazine, revolutionized psychiatry. The administration of these drugs to psychotic patients enabled locked wards to be opened, and permitted the release into the community of many patients, replacing the closed door of traditional psychiatry with *the revolving door*, through which the patients come and go. The essential point about this great innovation, however, is that it had nothing to do with treatment. Not for nothing has the major tranquillizer been called the *chemical strait-jacket*, for that is literally and precisely what it is. Previously the psychotic patient had been locked in a padded cell and/or strapped in a strait-jacket in order to suppress her dangerous or disturbing behaviour. Now, with the invention of the major tranquillizers, a far more effective and more 'civilized' method of doing exactly the same thing has been hit upon. The strait-jacket is not a treatment and nor, by the same token, is chlorpromazine. The major tranquillizers are not aimed at treating psychoses by attacking the alleged disease-process or even, as a symptomatic treatment, by attacking the symptoms themselves. If they were so intended we would expect the symptoms, the patient's abnormal behaviour, to be replaced by normal behaviour. But the drugs do not work like this. Rather, they work by reducing the patient to a semi-comatose, stupified zombie, capable of almost no behaviour whatever!

The consequence of this is that the debate about major tranquillizers is not at all a debate about treatment, whether this or that treatment is to be preferred, as psychiatrists would like it to be. It is a *moral* debate about whether psychotic behaviour should be forcibly abolished by *any* means. Such behaviour is often called 'disturbed'. R. D. Laing, amongst others, has argued that it is usually *we* who are disturbed by the patient's behaviour, rarely the patient. We find the be-

80

single crime perpetrated by psychologists in the name of science.

IQ testing had very practical beginnings. The first test was devised by the French psychologist, Alfred Binet, around the turn of the century, following a request from the Paris education authorities for a means of separating 'bright' children, who would profit from normal education, from 'dull' children, who would not. IQ tests have continued to offer very immediate benefits to the system. They formed an important part of the iniquitous 11+ selection examination, are still used in some comprehensive schools to determine streaming, and are routinely employed in the labelling of children, especially immigrant children, as ESN (educationally subnormal).

From these practical origins, the measurement of intelligence attracted the theoretical attention of a powerful school of British psychologists who were interested in the measurement of human characteristics and, particularly, in individual differences between them (see D4). This psychometric tradition was founded in the work of Francis Galton, himself a cousin of Darwin and a member of the British intellectual aristocracy at the end of the last century. It continues to occupy a prominent position in modern psychology. One of its fundamental assumptions is that human ability is inherited and relatively unaffected by the environment; consequently, success in life is primarily a justifiable reflection of this innate ability. These ideas follow by simple analogy from Darwin's principle of natural selection and are usually referred to as 'social Darwinism'. The politics of the psychometrics school were originally closely identified with *the eugenics movement*, the main proposal of which was that the human race should be improved by careful control of breeding and by ensuring that 'inferior' members of the race did not produce too many children. The reader will be aware that suggestions of this kind are a significant ingredient of fascism. I have included this background material to prepare for a discussion of the ideology of IQ testing.

The first thing to note is that intelligence testing is presented by its adherents as being a most respectable, highly rigorous branch of psychological science. This is very far from the truth. Even judged by its own limited standards, the area is riddled with circularities and inconsistencies which would make a respectable scientist blush. An initial source of distortion is the selection of test items. A basic assumption of intelligence testing is that IQ remains roughly constant over age, since it measures some intellectual potential of the individual fixed at birth. Longitudinal studies are conducted to show that this is indeed the case. However, this appearance of stability is quite spurious because the tests have been designed in the first place to ensure that changes with age do not occur; items which show fluctuations over time are dropped from the tests in the interests of 'reliability'. Thus, the finding that IQ remains constant merely reflects the fact that the test constructors have already defined intelligence, in their selection of test items, as something which does not change. Similarly, psychometricians set great store by the bell-shaped, normal distribution (see A8) of IQ scores. This is put forward as proving that intelligence is the biological characteristic it is alleged to be and is not much influenced by social factors. This is an even more blatant piece of circularity since the tests are constructed initially *in order* to fit the normal distribution.

The above examples suggest ways in which values creep in to the supposedly pure and value-free area of intelligence testing. When we come to consider the validation and standardization of the tests, the presence of values is quite clearly apparent. Psychometricians are very concerned with the *validity* of IQ tests, the proof that they do in fact measure what they are designed to measure – intelligence. A criterion often chosen for a new instrument is a high correlation with a well-established one, but the circularity of this procedure is obvious. The most frequent yardstick, however, is *educational success*. Therefore, what the test constructors mean by intelligence is ability to do well at school and, therefore, general intelligence is simply a pseudonym for *school intelligence*. Here is the method by which IQ testing bolsters the educational system it serves – by pretending that IQ is an objective measure of an inborn intelligence when it is really a measure of the extent to which the dominant values of society have been successfully learned. For although cognitive ability undoubtedly contributes to success at school, surely nobody would suggest that it is the *only* contributing factor. Motivational and social factors must play a large, if not an equal, part in determining academic success. But by presenting IQ as a measure of cognitive ability alone, the significance of social and motivational influences due, for example, to social class position, is lost sight of. Whatever might be wrong with the educational system is thus perpetuated in a pre-emptive definition of intelligence as that which the system at present aims to produce. As Ryan (1972) lucidly demonstrates, it is impossible to consider cognitive abilities in isolation from their social determinants. The 'illusion of objectivity' in IQ testing provides a dishonest, quasi-scientific apology for the class bias of the educational system.

Another route by which values enter intelligence testing is in the gathering of norms for IQ tests, the procedure known as *standardization*. I shall be dealing with this topic in the next chapter when the racist component of intelligence testing will be described. Let us consider here the less specific, harmful effects on our culture conveyed by the notion of IQ. We have already observed that the psychometrician's conception of intelligence is the extremely narrow one of doing well at school. The restricted nature of this perspective supports the very limited conception of 'education' accepted by most people in the culture. The rich associations of the word 'intelligence' which thankfully persist in the language, the many varied and exciting forms of human ability, the supreme achievements of cooperative human effort, these are all subordinated in the psychometric view to things like being good at arithmetic and spelling. More generally, IQ tests place heavy emphasis on logical problems which have only one solution to the exclusion of the many other creative methods we employ for the solution of real-life problems.

The villain of the piece is again the spectre of positivism (see F1 and F7). The psychometric impulse derives from the hope that psychology can arrive at the same kind of objective and static measurements of people that physics makes of the properties of things, so that people may be controlled as smoothly and efficiently as we imagine the physicist to control matter. But, as George Kelly has informed us, 'man is a form of motion'; he is *constantly* changing and developing. The attempt to describe him by fixed, thing-like measurements succeeds chiefly in pinning him down and retarding development. Rosenthal and Jacobson (1968) have shown clearly that children do poorly at school if their teachers have been led to expect, on the basis of IQ scores, that they will do poorly. Psychometric testing and the labelling which flows from it thus works as a classic example of the 'self-fulfilling prophecy'; its effect is to make come true that which it has predicted. What is more, the measurement of IQ has been received by the public (and by professionals like teachers and psychiatrists who should know better) as the same kind of measurement as used in physics, like measuring something with a ruler. In fact, it is nothing of the sort; it is only a way of ordering people relative to each other. It tells us nothing about the *properties* of a person, like the length of her arm or her age. Psychometricians have done little to discourage this misconception of the nature of psychological measurement because it accords with their own fantasies about making psychology into a science like physics. In this respect, they bear a heavy responsibility for encouraging human beings to think of themselves, and treat others, as mere aggregates of fixed, numerical quantities.

Clinical psychology

Clinical psychology first bought its way into mental hospitals by promising psychiatrists to provide an objective and quantitative back-up service for their diagnoses, in the form of psychological testing. To the extent, therefore, that clinical psychology supplies a pseudo-scientific aura of respectability to the pseudo-medical goings on of psychiatrists, most of the criticisms of psychiatry presented in the last chapter are relevant to it. Even if one accepts the legitimacy of psychiatric diagnosis, psychological testing contributes very little to it. As with IQ, the logic of diagnostic tests is circular because their ultimate validation is by the diagnosis itself. Hence, it cannot be claimed that they represent an improvement over diagnosis by psychiatrists since it is not possible for something to improve on what it is judged against. The main reason for their use is to conjure up a few arbitrary numbers so that everybody concerned can congratulate themselves on how 'objective' they are being. If the psychologist's report is at variance with what the doctor already believes about a patient, it is simply ignored.

Other kinds of psychological testing used in hospitals, such as the 'measurement' of personality, are subject to the same sorts of criticism as were levelled against IQ testing. The most frequently used personality tests are based on a static, 'trait' conception of personality which has been successfully discredited, if ever it needed to be, by Mischel (1968). They typically take the form of a thinly veiled disguise for derogatory descriptions of social deviance. Such tests do great damage to the interests of patients by attaching to them nasty labels which they have difficulty in shaking off. (For an instructive exposé of Cattell's infamous 16PF test, see *Humpty Dumpty*, 2.) We may account partially for the popularity of these tests by looking at the characteristics of psychologists themselves. Many of them, particularly of the older school, are frustrated physical scientists and mathematicians; they are far happier tapping up numbers on an electronic calculator than listening to the messy and boring problems of their fellow men and women. These psychologists spend much of their time in the childish construction of numerical castles in the air which have very little relevance to anything at all.

To be fair to clinical psychologists, few of them nowadays are content to be mere testers and it is often psychiatrists who try to restrict them to this role because of the threat they pose to medical hegemony. During the last ten years or so there has been a tremendous upsurge in psychological therapy and this is now the most prominent aspect of the clinical psychologist's work (see F3).

The most rapid expansion has been that of behaviour therapy. The enthusiasts of this relatively new approach reject the illness model of their psychiatric colleagues, at least as far as neuroses are concerned, and prefer to think in terms of maladaptive learned behaviours, after the principles of classical learning theory (see A3). From the radical point of view, it is essential to make the initial distinction between 'behaviour therapy', which is based on Pavlovian classical conditioning theory, and 'behaviour modification', based on the ideas of Skinner, which I have already discussed in Chapter 3. Behaviour therapy properly so called covers a wide range of therapeutic activities, not all of them objectionable in themselves. To be sure, it does include the entirely unacceptable electrical aversion treatment for homosexuals, which we will

113

look at in the next chapter. On the other hand, there can be no doubt that the model of the conditioned reflex, and the de-conditioning methods thought to derive from it, have proved most useful in the elimination of phobias and a few other kinds of problem. However, as the last sentence implies, this is not a triumph for the behaviouristic view of man. The actual methods employed in behaviour therapy bear very little relation to arid learning theories dreamt up in the animal laboratory, as anyone who has learned the one and done the other will know. We might even say that behaviour therapy works *in spite of* its foundations in animal learning theory, not because of them. Successful therapy is done by good thera-pists, those who have the necessary qualities of kindness, empathy, and practicality. Even the theorists of behaviour therapy are beginning to admit the importance of what they call 'cognitive' factors: the expectations the client has of therapy, how she construes her problem and her relationship with the therapist. Again, if behaviour therapy is successful, it will have countered the most harmful effects of the medical model, by ridding the patient of the notion that she has an 'illness' and by locating her problems in her present inter-action with the environment and not in her bloodstream or in events which happened before she was old enough to re-member them. The point I wish to make, though, is that radicals should beware of dismissing everything that goes on in the name of 'behaviour therapy' out of hand.

Having appeared to defend some uses of behaviour therapy, I should make clear that it does not go nearly far enough in its departure from the medical model. While there can be no serious objection to, say, enabling an agoraphobic client who has been afraid to go outside for years to once more leave the house, the client's problems do not end there. The learning theory construction of psychological problems has in common with the medical approach the misleading as-sumption that they lie within herself and not in her relation-ships with others and in society at large. To take the case of agoraphobia, my experience is that there is nearly always pre-sent a pronounced disharmony in personal and sexual rela-tionships. The client's frustration with her marriage is often due to the limited sex roles she and her husband occupy and this, in turn, is related to the roles imposed on men and women by capitalism and to the absence of creative possibilities offered to women by these roles. Behaviour therapy is as efficient as drug therapy in ignoring and disguising the social and political origins of these apparently personal problems. Clinical psychologists have invented new and better *means* to solve their clients' problems, but have paid insufficient attention to a rethinking of what those problems are, and to the subsequent formulation of new *ends* for therapy. Insofar as they have inherited the therapeutic goals of psychiatry – return to work, housewifery, respectability, conformity – clinical psychologists run the risk of becoming the vendors of a new, improved package of social control.

It seems likely that not a few psychologists are quite prepared to accept this risk. There is abroad in clinical psychology today a strong movement towards 'professionalism': the statutory recognition of psychologists' autonomy and their right to the status and prestige of other professionals, like medical doctors, architects, and lawyers. All this must be seen within the context of an unseemly and often degrading power-struggle between clinical psychologists and psychiatrists, which began with the newly found confidence of the former in their therapeutic role. The psychiatrists want to keep the psychologists down because the psychologists, transparently, want to step into the psychiatrists' shoes (and their salaries!). This ambition is, in my view, quite mistaken. There can be no argument about who should be in charge of hospitals – doctors, because hospitals are places where sick people go to be treated. When psychologists insist, quite rightly, that their clients are not ill, they should draw the obvious conclusion and start pressing for the means to conduct 'clinical' psychology outside medicine.

Even if the psychologists succeeded in emancipating themselves from medicine there would still be great dangers in professionalism. I have consistently used the word 'client' when referring to the recipients of clinical psychology because it is an obvious improvement over 'patient'; further, it has the added implication that the client determines the goals of therapy, and no satisfactory alternative springs readily to mind. However, it has the serious disadvantage that it evokes the role of psychologist as professional expert. The main objection to behaviour therapy as it is practised, and to other

115

forms of psychological therapy, is that it is a form of inter-action in which one person *does something to* another, in virtue of superior knowledge and skills. It thus has the effect of distancing the therapist from the client, creating a new category of 'us' and 'them' and disqualifying one human be-ing from entering into a mutual problem-solving relationship *with* another. A naive commitment to psychological therapy inhibits psychologists from inquiring into their own experi-ence, questioning their own development and from relating this personal experience to that of their clients. Because of this, it confers upon psychologists the status of expert in an impersonal, technical, and manipulative relationship with a helpless other – helpless unless helped by the psychologist. The truth is that the practice of behaviour therapy is very simple; practically anybody could do it. Moreover, the crucial ingredients of successful psychotherapy, as we shall see in the next chapter, are not so much technical skills as *personal qualities*. One of the more heartening features of recent clinical psychology is the growth of *a personalist movement* within the discipline, which has the aim, amongst others, of weakening the role-related restrictions of the therapeutic relationship and of thereby advancing the *democratization* of psychological therapies. It remains to be seen whether this movement can divert the drive towards professionalism in clinical psychology. For let us be perfectly clear what pro-fessionalism means. *The professional is someone who takes away from the people knowledge and skills which rightfully belong to them.*

6
Psychology and the oppressed

Continuing with the aim of filling in the gaps in our coverage of radical psychology, I now intend to present the views of some oppressed groups of people who have implicated psychology and psychiatry in their accusations against society in general (see too B5). I will deal first with women, homosexuals, and blacks, and then conclude with a somewhat larger oppressed group.

Women

It would be encouraging to think that, by this stage in the book, the reader can anticipate the crux of women's objections to psychology. It is that psychology reinforces, both theoretically and practically, the very restricted roles and limited life-opportunities of women in our society. The typical description of female personality to be found in psychology books, usually written by men, is an extraordinary mixture of tolerant amusement and patronizing contempt: a transparent copy of the worst kind of stereotype held of women by men. They are depicted as weak, silly, dependent, childish creatures, spending all their energy trying to be attractive enough to grab a man so that they can spend the rest of their lives attempting to gratify him. Being a good wife and mother is put forth as being woman's true, 'natural' role and the fulfilment of her 'basic' nature. The tragedy is, of course, that this stereotype has a ring of truth about it. The question is *why* some women are like this. Is it because of some inborn personality structure, based on biological differences from men, as most psychological theories suggest, or is it the result of cultural expectations, themselves heavily backed up by psychologists, as to what women's place in the social order should be? Naomi Weisstein (1973) shows that there is not a shred of evidence to suppose that *all* so-called psychological differences between men and women are not the product of social learning experiences, in which women are moulded into what society requires of them. Under the guise of exploring woman's basic nature, positivistic psychology gives a pseudo-scientific endorsement to current societal attitudes towards women in a male-dominated society. Rather than showing any interest in what might really be 'basic' to women – their unfettered potential to develop intellectually and creatively in a free society – it attempts merely to orchestrate capitalism's campaign of keeping women firmly in their place.

The roots of sexist psychology are located in Freudian theory (see D3). Although there is much that is timeless in psychoanalysis, important parts of the theory were deeply influenced by the times in which Freud lived and by his own authoritarian and patriarchal character. This is especially true of his account of female psychology. The most obnoxious concept is that of 'penis envy'. What we are invited to believe is that, upon discovering boys to have penises which they do not possess, little girls reach the conclusion that they must have been castrated and this gives them a life-long envy of the male sexual organ and a deep-seated feeling of inferiority to men. Indeed, women *are* intellectually and morally inferior. Little boys are able to resolve 'the oedipus complex', in which they are said to be in competition with their fathers for their mother's love, by backing down from the father's threats of castration and identifying with him and his moral code. This is the origin of the 'superego'. Having already been castrated, as it were, girls do not get this opportunity and therefore grow up into moral imbeciles. Apart from these specific ingredients, there runs throughout Freud's work a characterization of women as the passive and accommodating background to the active and aggressive male; there is also the steady implication that a woman's sexual function in

118

pleasing the male is, and should be, the almost exclusive pre-occupation of her life. (See the article by Magagona in *Rat, Myth and Magic*.) It seems scarcely credible that all this drivel, revealing as it does an obvious fear of and hostility to-wards women on Freud's part, should have been accepted as gospel by orthodox psychoanalysis for so many years.

✗ Koedt (1974) describes a related aspect of Freudian sexist mythology which has had a very harmful effect on many women's lives. I refer to what has become known as *the myth of the vaginal orgasm*. Freud maintained that female orgasm by stimulation of the clitoris, the female counterpart of the penis, was just an adolescent phenomenon and that at puberty a woman should transfer the centre of erotic sensitivity to the vagina in order to achieve a parallel but more mature orgasm. It is only recently that psychological research has shown this notion of 'the double orgasm' to be completely without founda-tion (Masters and Johnson, 1966). The ideological significance of this blatant piece of male chicanery, says Koedt, is that it makes the whole object of fucking for the woman the pleasure of her male partner, since men usually reach orgasm in vaginal penetration. It still happens that women who report that they cannot achieve the non-existent vaginal orgasm are labelled as frigid by psychiatrists and in need of psychiatric treatment, at the expense of enormous damage to their self-conceptions and to their relationships with men. What Koedt regards as even more outrageous is that countless women must have been badgered by male psychiatrists and other men into acknow-ledging the experience of a kind of orgasm which modern research has proved conclusively to be a myth. *Freudian psy-chology is seriously implicated in the sexual oppression of women.*

Psychiatry as a whole is implicated in the more general oppression of women in society. Women supply over 60 per cent of all psychiatric patients. How are we to account for this significantly higher incidence of 'mental illness' in women than in men? Psychiatrists account for it, implicitly if not explicitly, by assuming the female of the species to be 'the weaker vessel', less able than the tougher and more logical male to withstand the pressures of living. I do not ever re-member hearing a psychiatrist assert that this greater prone-ness was due to the greater frustration and emptiness in most women's lives. As with other forms of treatment, the criterion for successful treatment of women is an adjustment to society, to what psychiatrists see at their naturally ordained function as child-rearers and husband-pleasers. To liberate themselves, women have found it necessary to decline psychiatry's offer of help for their problems in order *to help themselves* in the solidarity of the Women's Movement.

I hinted earlier that capitalism has a vested interest in the sexual and social oppression of women. This is because the woman is the nucleus of *the nuclear family*, the centre around which the other family members gravitate. The nuclear family of husband, wife, and offspring is essential to capitalism for several reasons. First, it breaks society down into small units so that industry can reduplicate its products in every household and hugely increase the consumption of goods which would otherwise become unnecessary. Secondly, the family set-up creates the competitive ethos of 'keeping up with the Jones's', thus hindering people from joining together in the mutual understanding of their exploitation and the collective action needed to put an end to it. Thirdly, in comparison with the school, the family unit works as a less organized, but in some ways more effective, means of ideologizing the child into a compliant acceptance of the exploitation and violence of capitalism and the alienated conditions of life it requires. The importance of the family to capitalism is the real reason behind the double standards of sexual morality applied to men and women; the 'unfaithfulness' of the wife is so much more dangerous than that of the husband because it threatens the precious family structure on which capitalism depends.

The ideological propensity of the family has been a favourite target of attack for the existential psychiatrists. For example, David Cooper (1972), a close collaborator of Laing, has written a book called *The Death of the Family*, which advocates the abandonment of the family way of life and its replacement by the anti-family of communal living. Recent radical criticisms of the family must be related to a strong movement in the counter-culture, which has already created many urban and rural communes all over the country. The aim of the communards is to experiment with new forms of living together in preparation for a major change in the economic structure of society, in which communal living may become a possibility for everyone. They also achieve by this means a greater personal liberation from the tyranny of the capitalist order and this is especially true of women.

Gays

In our discussion of the myth of mental illness and of the moral and political nature of psychiatric intervention, we might well have used the example of homosexuality as a test-case, for here all the relevant issues are starkly revealed. Homosexuals comprise what is probably the most consistently and savagely oppressed minority in society, and psychiatry valiantly supports their subjection by labelling homosexuality as an illness (see F3). The vaguest but most persistent justification for denigrating this particular form of social deviance in this way is that it is 'unnatural'. But we have seen time and again in this book that what is regarded as natural is simply a reflection of prevailing norms. Many human societies have found homosexuality a perfectly natural part of the social order and, if it is a disease, then it must be the most common known to man, since it has been estimated that about 5 per cent of the population is gay, either overtly or, more often, in secret. The truth is that our society fears and persecutes the homosexual because of the threat he or she poses to a sexist and male-dominated social structure. Szasz (1970) has described the homosexual as *the model psychiatric scapegoat*.

The chief contribution of psychiatry to this persecution is that, by inviting the harrassed and despised homosexual to see himself as sick, he is thereby allowed the soft option of admitting there is something wrong with him. This assuages to some extent the guilt imposed on him but also adroitly side-steps a debate about human freedom and defuses any open conflict his defiant homosexuality might provoke. Neither should the reader be confused by talk of the 'causes' of homosexuality, because the search for causes presupposes that there exists a problem to be solved – apart from society's oppression. After all, nobody bothers to look for the 'causes' of heterosexuality, do they? The many and varied theories which have been proposed by psychiatrists and psychologists to account for homosexuality – hormonal, oedipal, social learning, and so on – are all irrelevant to the decision to define a form of social deviance as an illness in need of cure.

It should be conceded that some liberal psychiatrists agree with the above analysis and reject the illness model of homosexuality. But what, they plaintively ask, are we to do with the homosexual who requests treatment? We surely cannot refuse him; our medical ethics would not allow it. The pertinent question is, why are these psychiatrists offering treatment in the first place? If homosexuality is not an illness, what have doctors to do with it? The very fact that the *medically* qualified are considered authorities on a *moral* debate beguiles unhappy homosexuals into thinking that their sexual preference is *in itself* a cause of unhappiness. They are never informed of the many homosexuals who have achieved stable and satisfying relationships with others. Thus, Gay Liberation do not want a *reformed* medical attitude to homosexuality; they want no attitude at all. They do not want psychiatrists to *correct* their chapters on homosexuality, but to omit them. The doctor consulted by a confused and lonely homosexual should suggest that he contact one of the many Gay organizations where he may find the courage and pride to live openly as a homosexual. All the above remarks apply without change to lesbians and examples of their views may be found in *The Radical Therapist* (RT Collective, 1974).

Easily the most appalling feature of clinical psychology's involvement in the area is the use of aversion therapy (see F1 and F3). This has now become the 'treatment of choice' for homosexuality in most hospitals. Typically, the patient is asked to bring along photographs of people he or she finds attractive, possibly including past or present lovers, and is then given a protracted course of electric shocks or nausea-inducing drugs while looking at them. In more sophisticated versions, pictures of heterosexual sex symbols are shown to the patient just after the cessation of electric shock, thus associating relief from pain with sex objects acceptable to the psychologist. Obviously, psychologists will insist that they give aversion therapy only to those who ask for it, but the hypocrisy of justifying any form of treatment for homosexuality in this way has already been mentioned. Moreover, there is considerable irony in the appeal by behaviourists to *voluntary* requests for treatment when they rarely tire of proclaiming free-will to be an illusion. The most serious objection to aversion therapy, however, is revealed by its theoretical underpinning. Enthusiasts of the approach will inform you that it is essentially a more efficient and scientifically controlled method for delivering the aversive conditioning for maladaptive behaviours which is found in society generally. Therefore, what the therapists are doing when they shock or nauseate their patients is punishing them, irrespective of whether or not the patient has been sufficiently bullied by society into asking for punishment. What the aversion therapists seem to be saying is: 'Since the punishment already inflicted on these poor devils has clearly failed to work, we will cheerfully attempt to complete the process.' As a Gay Lib. pamphlet (no. 1) poignantly remarks: 'Ours is a society which claims to uphold romantic love – yet allows doctors to induce people to vomit over pictures of those they love.' We must conclude, I think, that the punishment of homosexuals by aversion therapy is *a more refined and legalized form of queer-bashing*.

Blacks

There are probably many ways in which psychology has lent its assistance to the oppression of black people. Nevertheless in this section I will concentrate on one particular claim which has been made by psychologists – that blacks are intellectually inferior to whites (see too B5 and D4). This is not to say that other aspects of psychology's involvement in racial discrimination are not important, but that the fierce controversy which has raged over the intelligence issue in the last few years has dwarfed all other considerations.

I have already pointed out in Chapter 5 the intimate connections between the hereditarian view of human intelligence and the political philosophy of the eugenics movement. During the 1920s, this movement used the results of intelligence testing to influence the American immigration and naturalization laws, creating a preference for pure, 'Nordic' stock, at the expense of inferior 'Alpine' and 'Mediterranean' types. It also succeeded in getting compulsory sterilization for the 'feeble-minded, criminals and paupers' on to the statute-books of several American states. Later, during the 1930s, when open support for fascism became less popular than it had been, the eugenicists were considerably embarrassed by the close correspondence of their views to the policy of the Nazi party. This then is the political heritage of 'the new eugenics movement', led in the USA by Jensen and by Eysenck in Britain. The kernel of fascism is the assertion that important differences in overt human behaviour, and especially in human ability, are determined by inherited, biological differences between races. This is also the thesis of the distinguished professors mentioned above. When radicals call the views of these men fascist, they are not being hot-headed and woolly-minded political 'extremists'; they are accurately describing their scientific hypotheses.

The question of black intellectual inferiority is, of course, a matter of evidence. That should go without saying. Nobody seriously disputes that blacks do in fact score lower on IQ tests than whites; the average gap is usually estimated at about fifteen points. What is in dispute is *why* they show this deficit and what it *means* that they do. We have seen in the preceding chapter that IQ is not a measure of 'intelligence'. It is merely a means of predicting who will do well at school and who will succeed in life. As such, it favours the rich and privileged and discriminates against the poor. In as much as blacks are almost always members of the working class, IQ tests work to their disadvantage in this way. However, the most outstanding source of discrimination arises in the standardization of the tests. In this procedure, the test is given to a large sample of the population and is then adjusted, by the inclusion of some items and the omission of others and by a suitable weighting of points awarded, so that the mean score of each age group comes out at 100, with a set standard deviation, usually 15 (see A8). Thus, if the mean of the standardization sample is above 100, the test is made easier, and if it is below 100, more difficult. The sample employed is meant to be *representative* of the general population in question, for otherwise certain sections of the population would be left out and the test might be biased against them. Perhaps the reader will not be too surprised when I inform her that, despite the golden rule of representativeness, the two most commonly used tests in the world, the Stanford–Binet and the Wechsler Intelligence Scale for Children, were standardized *on whites only* (see test manuals). It seems somewhat unfair, to put it very mildly, to expect one cultural group to perform well on a test for which the *standards* have been set by another. As Ryan (1972) puts it, we may compare blacks and whites on IQ tests, but in doing so we are not comparing black and white intelligence. We are seeing how blacks do on tests of white intelligence.

Not only are IQ tests constructed by whites and standardized on whites, they are also given by whites. It has been known for some time that a black person's measured IQ is on average 6 points higher if the test is given by another black, than if it is given by a white. The conclusion from this appears to be that the testing situation is a microcosm of the total society. The black filling in whitey's IQ test sees it as a part of the racial prejudice and injustice he is confronted with every day of his life. In this, he is correct! (see Watson, 1972).

The clearest illustration of the ideological significance of IQ comes from the procedure known as *restandardization.* Before 1937, the mean of women's scores on the Stanford–Binet was about 10 points lower than that of men. (This is another example of the distorted validation of the tests. After the age of thirteen or fourteen, girls do less well at school because being clever is considered unladylike. They also do less well on the major criterion for adult tests, success in life, for reasons which have nothing to do with intelligence.) At any rate, the decision was taken to restandardize the test to eliminate this difference. Existing items were dropped and fresh ones inserted until women did as well as men. Now, the question we have to ask is this: why has not a similar restandardization been carried out to eliminate the difference between blacks and whites? The answer the psychometricians would give is that to do so would lower the predictive efficiency of the test. Precisely! For what IQ tests aim to predict, and therefore serve to support, is the much greater chances of success in life for whites than blacks. Interestingly enough, the decision to abolish differences in IQ between men and women *did* lower the predictive efficiency of the Stanford–Binet, because it removed a source of bias from the test which continued to exist in society. Exactly the same arguments could be applied to the gap in mean IQ between the middle and working classes. The decision whether or not to re-standardize, to eliminate known differences between social groups, is a purely political decision, reflecting the political values of the test-constructors. I trust the reader has been left in no doubt that *the IQ test is a weapon of ideological warfare.*

There are many other criticisms that could be made of the concept of intelligence as used by psychologists and of the nature of IQ testing, but space is limited. Suffice it to say that the reader should *not* accept the parrot-like assertion that intelligence is 80 per cent inherited. This statement is extremely contentious, to say the least. Moreover, when the hereditarians minimize the effects of the environment on intelligence, their concept of the environment is a crudely simplistic one; it takes no account, for example, of the relation between nutritional deficiency and impaired cognitive development (see C1). Finally, one most important point needs to be made. The debate about black and white intelligence is not an irrelevant academic exercise. Jensen's arguments were used in America to support the closing down of the Headstart programme, which was designed to give under-privileged black children compensatory education. Careful assessment of the results of this programme shows that it did *not* fail in its aim of emancipating black people from their Sambo-like self-conceptions and the apathetic hopelessness of their situation. The reason it was closed down is because it represented a threat to the economic domination of the white middle class. The pronouncements of Jensen, Eysenck, and their followers provide a superficially respectable and highly quotable string of rationalizations for the resurgence of racism in America and Britain. The saga of black IQ is yet another sordid chapter in the enslavement and exploitation of black people by white. (For a thorough and illuminating review of this entire area, see the Progressive Labour Party pamphlet *Racism, IQ and the Class Society.*)

Everybody

The idea that everybody is oppressed in our kind of society, even those we usually call the oppressors, gives me the opportunity to present some important elements of radical psychology which have not so far been described. For any justice to be done to the three topics below, they would require at least a book to themselves, even for an elementary introduction. All I can do here is simply point to their existence and once again suggest further reading.

Human potential

During the last few years there has spread from America to Britain a proliferation of new therapies – encounter groups of various sorts, sensitivity groups, gestalt therapy, primal therapy, bioenergetics, and re-evaluation counselling, to name but a few of the best known (see F3). All these therapies can be included under the rubric of *the human potential movement*, which I first mentioned in Chapter 2. Most of them are not aimed specifically at 'sick' or 'neurotic' people, but at all of us. In other words, the message of the movement is that we are all neurotic, because we live in a world which requires unreal forms of living and the repression of our real feelings. There is an important difference between *op*pression and *re*pression. Oppression is what somebody does to you; repression is what you do to yourself. The way in which society exerts its oppression is chiefly by forcing people to repress themselves. The common aim of the new therapies is to create social situations, usually involving groups of people, in which they may relate to each other more honestly in ways which are not normally allowed. By doing so, they come to break through the barriers of their repression, are enabled to experience and express genuine feelings and emotions, and begin to explore their true potential in more open and fruitful relationships.

It is easy to sneer at the human potential movement. For one thing, there is no doubt that some smooth operators have already made not a few quick bucks out of it. As I hinted earlier, some of the fattest fees are earned in support of capitalist industry. There is also no doubt that the therapies used have a limited middle-class application and that some of the things that go on under the name of therapy can descend to the level of silly party games or a kind of disingenuous Postman's Knock. More crucially, while there is much talk of society's culpability in the creation of neurosis, there is seldom any attempt to reach the degree of *political* consciousness which is the necessary precursor of an actual liberation from society's oppression. Nevertheless, on balance, I feel that to concentrate on these obvious shortcomings would be to do the movement an injustice and that there are other, more interesting aspects of it which deserve our serious consideration.

I will not attempt a description of the new therapies here since this may be found elsewhere (see F3, D3, B1). Still the most prominent type of activity is that known as the *encounter group* (see Carl Rogers and John Rowan, *Psychology Today*, 1975, no. 2). To my mind however, the therapy which stands the best chance of avoiding the pitfalls I mentioned above is *re-evaluation counselling*. For one thing, its founder, Harvey Jackins, has explicitly stated that economic exploitation is the basis of all oppression. But he believes that the struggle against this exploitation must go hand in hand with a personal liberation from social conditioning. Again, I will not describe what goes on in this therapy or the theory of human functioning on which it is based, since it is possible that it is the *democratic form* of re-evaluation counselling which is its most exciting feature. The democratization of therapy began with Carl Rogers' 'client-centred therapy', which did much to combat the mystique and elitism of psychotherapies derived from Freudian psychology. Subsequently, Truax and Carkhuff (1967) demonstrated that the essential attributes of successful therapists, irrespective of what 'school' they belonged to, were the personal qualities of empathy, warmth, and genuineness. Lay men and women who possessed these qualities, but who had no experience or knowledge of psychological therapy, could be taught in a relatively short time to be effective therapists. Jackins' method has completed this development by abolishing the distinction between therapist and therapized altogether. This is why the method is sometimes known as 'peer co-counselling'; the therapy is conducted between equals who take it in turn to listen to and encourage the discharge of repressed emotions by each other. After the basic skills have been learned in a group situation, they may be passed on to growing numbers of others without the interference and domination of the dreaded expert. This form of therapy contains interesting social and political possibilities.

Wilhelm Reich and the sexual revolution

An important influence on the human potential movement has been Wilhelm Reich, but to understand his work it is necessary to go back to the founder of psychoanalysis. The perspective which sees neurosis as a condition of everyone in society originated with Freud, as did the accompanying concept of *repression*. Freud intended this term in a highly technical sense I will not be able to discuss here but, very roughly, the idea is this. Freud's theory is about *conflict*. The basic form of conflict is between the individual and society, between the individual's need to satisfy the demands of sexual and aggressive biological instincts and the need of civilization that these instincts be kept under tight rein. Therefore, the child is taught to channel instinctual desires into socially recognized and approved modes of expression. For the rest, the child learns to repress; that is, he comes to activate defences, which are themselves unconscious, in order to block awareness of the now disturbing instinctual impulses. In adult life, it is the struggle of repressed instincts to find outlets which creates the neuroses characterizing the normal member of society.

Despite his assault on hypocrisy and the bizarre attitudes to sex of his time, Freud's vision of society was a distinctly pessimistic one (see F3). He could not imagine a future society which would allow more freedom for the expression of individual needs and, hence, regarded man's neurotic condition as a permanent and inevitable feature of his existence. The task of reconciling the individual and society was left to Reich, and this makes him the first thinker to take seriously the revolutionary implications of Freud's work. Specifically, Reich attempted the marriage of psychoanalysis and Marxism; he tried to envisage what a society would be like in which sexual repression was not an inevitability and found it to be a socialist society (see B5). Whether or not Reich's attempt was successful is beside the present point. He began a tradition of thought which rejects Freud's gloomy interpretation of his own great insights and strives towards the discovery of a form of social organization which does not *excessively* prohibit the expression of individual needs and desires and in which greater personal freedom is not incompatible with civic order.

To some extent, Reich's influence on the human potential movement has been direct. This is especially true of the concept of 'character-armour', in which a person's habitual orientation to life is often seen as a defence against repressed impulses. He also contributed to the emphasis on physical, non-verbal means of expression and communication. But it would be a mistake to think that sex was the main preoccupation of the new movement, as it was for Reich. Human needs in a search of fulfilment continue long after sexual needs have been satisfied. Perhaps the chief affinity between Reich's thought and that of the humanistic psychologists is a sense of optimism regarding man's potential. Those tendencies which society now demands that we repress are not all the nasty and brutish impulses Freud imagined them to be, but include also the very possibilities in human nature necessary to man's continued survival on earth.

Marx and alienation

It is likely that the reader thinks of Marx exclusively in terms of the economic determinism associated with his greatest work, *Capital*. However, it was only after World War Two that Marx's earlier writings began to be translated and published and this early work has considerably broadened our understanding of the body of his thought. It reveals that Marx, besides being an economist, sociologist, historian, and philosopher, can also be called a humanistic psychologist. Some Marxists have rejected what they consider to be the immature and 'unscientific' ramblings of the younger Marx as having little connection with the later period in his thought. But many others have seen a strong thread of continuity between the two – a continuity which integrates man's personal experience of life under capitalism with the great social and economic forces which make it up. The most important concept in this earlier period is one we have already encountered several times in the book – *alienation* (see B5).

Marx's psychology fits well with the requirements of the non-positivistic science of man outlined in Chapter 2. Man is regarded as active rather than passive, a creature who self-consciously regulates his own activity rather than being blindly driven by mechanistic forces outside his control. At the same time, he is a social animal whose consciousness of the world and activity in it are embedded in the social structure he inhabits; the individual's psychology reflects the stage of economic and political development of the times in which he lives. For Marx, the objective essence of man is his *self-creativity*. Man is distinguished from the rest of the animal kingdom by being the only animal who self-consciously transforms himself as a result of his own *labour*. In other words, man changes himself by simultaneously changing his external world. Thus, Marx's use of the word 'labour' is far wider than its normal meaning; it refers to man's creative interaction with Nature. This is man's *species-character* – the characteristic of man that makes him what he is.

What happens to this species-character in the capitalist mode of production? Capitalism is distinguished by a particular kind of division of labour, one in which the tools mankind uses to work upon the environment, *the means of production*, are owned by a few people who then employ many others to do the work. Under this system, labour has become a commodity, something which is bought and sold. The fact that it is bought for less than it is worth is precisely what enables the profits to be made which sustain capitalism, and this constitutes the exploitation of the many by the few. Marx never denied that this form of property relations had given great benefits to the race, through the tremendous release of productive capacity. But he also maintained that it had resulted in very detrimental effects on the worker, what he called 'a certain mental and physical crippling'. The concept of alienation refers first to the relationship between the producer and the means of production. Whereas previously men used and dominated the tools of their labour, under capitalism the machine now uses and dominates them. The worker, instead of being a living creator, now becomes another kind of *thing*, a mere appendage of the production process. Moreover, since he does not own the means of production, he takes no part in deciding how and to what ends they shall be used.

Secondly, the products which should be the fruit of the worker's labour and which contain something of himself, are taken away from him and, indeed, become an alien power over him. Man is dominated by the things he produces and by the economic conditions he has created to produce them. The results of man's labour have acquired a power and life of their own and, as Marx says, 'the lord of creation has become the slave of his creation'.

Thirdly, not only is the producer alienated from his work and from his products, he is also alienated from other producers. The constant drive for profit which is inevitable under capitalism, and the struggle for survival this brings about, separates men from their fellow-men and puts them in egotistical competition with each other. The working class obviously does worst out of the system, but all are afflicted with the passion for having, the distorted experience of life which sees the possession of material goods as its primary goal.

Lastly, the species-character of man, the human creativity which should be the *end* of his existence, has become a mere *means* of survival. Man works to live, rather than lives to work. As Marx said: 'The problem is to organize the empirical world in such a manner that man experiences in it the truly human, becomes accustomed to experience himself as man, to assert his true individuality.'

The great paradox of all this is that Marx believed that man is truly human only in freedom from physical necessity. He did not despise industry and technology in themselves but only the irrational and destructive uses to which they had been put. We are now in a situation where the exploitation of the worker by the capitalist has been submerged under the exploitation of the poor, underdeveloped Third World by the rich, industrialized nations. Yet, for the first time in human history, if man's enormous energy, limitless ingenuity, and *existing* technological capacity were put to rational use, the virtual elimination of want *and* of alienation could become a real possibility for the entire race.

Further Reading

Note: Where a book or magazine is relevant to more than one chapter, it has been listed once only.

General

Brown, Phil (ed.) (1973) *Radical Psychology*. London: Tavistock Publications.

Hampden-Turner, Charles (1971) *Radical Man*. London: Duckworth.

Heavy Daze magazine, from COPE, 146 Great Western Road, London W11.

Humpty Dumpty magazine, from 28 Redbourne Avenue, London N3 2BS.

Radical Therapist Collective (1974) *The Radical Therapist*. Harmondsworth: Penguin.

Rat, Myth and Magic pamphlet, still available from Nigel Armistead, 32 Parkholme Road, London, E.8.

Red Rat magazine, from 42 Essendine Mansions, Essendine Road, London W.9.

Self and Society magazine, from 62 Southwark Bridge Road, London SE1 0AS.

Chapter 2: Positivism and Psychology

Armistead, Nigel (ed.) (1974) *Reconstructing Social Psychology*. Harmondsworth: Penguin.

Bannister, D. and Fransella, Fay (1971) *Inquiring Man*. Harmondsworth: Penguin.

Kolakowski, Leszek (1972) *Positivist Philosophy*. Harmondsworth: Penguin.

Manis, J. G. and Meltzer, B. N. (1972) *Symbolic Interaction*. Boston: Allyn and Bacon.

Wann, T. W. (ed.) (1964) *Behaviourism and Phenomenology*. Chicago: Univ. Chicago Press.

Chapter 3: Values and Ideology

Ingleby, David (1972) Ideology and the human sciences. In Trevor Pateman (ed.) *Counter Course*. Harmondsworth: Penguin.

Laing, R. D. (1967) *The Politics of Experience*. Harmondsworth: Penguin.

Marcuse, Herbert (1964) *One Dimensional Man*. London: Routledge and Kegan Paul.

Taylor, Ian and Taylor, Laurie (eds) (1973) *Politics and Deviance*. Harmondsworth: Penguin.

Young, Jock (1971) *The Drugtakers*. London: Paladin.

Chapter 4: Psychiatry and Anti-psychiatry

Boyers, R. and Orrill, R. (eds) (1972) *Laing and Anti-Psychiatry*. Harmondsworth: Penguin.

Cooper, David (1967) *Psychiatry and Anti-Psychiatry*. London: Tavistock Publications.

Goffman, Erving (1968) *Asylums*. Harmondsworth: Penguin.

Scheff, T. J. (1966) *Being Mentally Ill*. Chicago: Aldine Press.

Szasz, T. S. (1970) *Ideology and Insanity*. New York: Doubleday.

Chapter 5: Applied Psychology

Reimer, Everett (1971) *School is Dead*. Harmondsworth: Penguin.

Richardson, Ken and Spears, David (eds) (1972) *Race, Culture and Intelligence*. Harmondsworth: Penguin.

Brown, Norman (1959) *Life Against Death.* London: Routledge and Kegan Paul.

Fischer, Ernst (1973) *Marx in His Own Words.* Harmondsworth: Penguin.

Gay Liberation Pamphlet No. 1 (1973) *Psychiatry and the Homosexual* from Rising Free, 197 Kings Cross Road, London, N.1.

Maslow, Abraham (1973) *The Farther Reaches of Human Nature.* Harmondsworth: Penguin.

Millett, Kate (1971) *Sexual Politics.* London: Rupert Hart-Davis.

Progressive Labour Party pamphlet (1974) *Racism, IQ and the Class Society* from Humpty Dumpty, 28 Redbourne Avenue, London N3 2BS.

References and
Name Index

The numbers in italics following each entry refer to page numbers within this book

Bateson, G., Jackson, D., Haley, J. and Weakland, J. (1956) Toward a theory of schizophrenia. *Behav. Sci. 1*: 251–64. *96*

Becker, Howard S. (1963) *Outsiders: Studies in the Sociology of Deviance*. New York: Free Press. *71*

Broadbent, D. E. (1973) *In Defence of Empirical Psychology*. London: Methuen. *24–5*

Brown, Phil (ed.) (1973) *Radical Psychology*. London: Tavistock Publications. *9*

Cooper, David (1972) *The Death of the Family*. Harmondsworth: Penguin. *120*

Eysenck, H. J. (1969) The technology of consent. *New Scientist*, 26 June: 688–90. *46–7*

Eysenck, H. J. (1970) *Crime and Personality*. (revised ed.) London: Paladin. *52, 104*

Foucault, Michel (1967) *Madness and Civilization*. London: Tavistock Publications. *98*

Goffman, Erving (1968) *Asylums*. Harmondsworth: Penguin. *72, 85–7, 88*

Harré, Rom (1974) Blueprint for a new science. In Nigel Armistead (ed.) *Reconstructing Social Psychology*. Harmondsworth: Penguin. *22*

Harré, Rom and Secord, P. F. (1972) *The Explanation of Social Behaviour*. Oxford: Blackwell. *17–18*

Hollingshead, A. B. and Redlich, F. R. (1958) *Social Class and Mental Illness*. New York: Wiley. *74*

Ingleby, David (1972) Ideology and the human sciences. In Trevor Pateman (ed.) *Counter Course*. Harmondsworth: Penguin. *45–6*

Koedt, Anne (1974) The myth of the vaginal orgasm. In Radical Therapist Collective *The Radical Therapist*, Harmondsworth: Penguin. *119*

Kolakowski, Leszek (1972) *Positivist Philosophy*. Harmondsworth: Penguin. *44*

Laing, R. D. (1959) *The Divided Self*. London: Tavistock Publications. *93–4, 95–6*

Laing, R. D. (1961) *The Self and Others*. London: Tavistock Publications. *96*

Laing, R. D. (1967) *The Politics of Experience*. Harmondsworth: Penguin. *54, 97–8, 99*

Laing, R. D. and Esterson, A. (1964) *Sanity, Madness and the Family*. London: Tavistock Publications. *96–7*

Maddison, Simon (1973) Mindless militants? Psychiatry and the university. In Ian Taylor and Laurie Taylor (eds) *Politics and Deviance*. Harmondsworth: Penguin. *51*

Maher, Brendan A. (1970) *Principles of Psychopathology*. New York: McGraw-Hill. *83*

Marcuse, Herbert (1964) *One Dimensional Man*. London: Routledge and Kegan Paul. *43*

Masters, W. H. and Johnson, V. E. (1966) *Human Sexual Response*. Boston: Little Brown. *119*

Matza, David (1969) *Becoming Deviant*. New York: Prentice-Hall. *35–6*

Mayer-Gross, W., Slater, E. and Roth, M. (1960) *Clinical Psychiatry*. London: Cassell. *75–6*

McLeod, R. B. (1964) Phenomenology: a challenge to experimental psychology. In T. W. Wann (ed.) *Behaviourism and Phenomenology*. Chicago: Univ. Chicago Press. *36*

Mischel, W. (1968) *Personality and Assessment*. New York: Wiley. *113*

Orne, M. T. (1962) On the social psychology of the psychological experiment: with particular reference to demand characteristics and their implications. *Amer. Psychol.* 58: 277–99. *32*

Pearce, Frank (1973) Crime, corporations and the American social order. In Ian Taylor and Laurie Taylor (eds) *Politics and Deviance*. Harmondsworth: Penguin. *105*

Radical Therapist Collective (1974) *The Radical Therapist*. Harmondsworth: Penguin. *101, 107, 122*

Rogers, Carl (1975) What happens in an encounter group? *Psychology Today*, no. 2 (May): 21–6. *35, 128*

Rosenhan, D. L. (1973) On being sane in insane places. *Science* 19: 250–8. *65–6*

Rosenthal, R. (1966) *Experimenter Effects in Behavioural Research*. New York: Appleton-Century-Crofts. *32–3*

Rosenthal, R. and Jacobson, L. (1968) *Pygmalion in the Classroom: Teacher Expectation and Pupils' Intellectual Development*. New York: Holt, Rinehart and Winston. *111–12*

Rowan, John (1975) Other ways of meeting. *Psychology Today*, no. 2 (May): 27–30. *128*

Ryan, Joanna (1972) IQ—The illusion of objectivity. In Ken Richardson and David Spears (eds) *Race, Culture and Intelligence*. Harmondsworth: Penguin. *111, 125*

Sartre, J. P. (1957) *Being and Nothingness*. (trans. by H. E. Barnes) London: Methuen. *26*

Scheff, T. J. (1966) *Being Mentally Ill: A Sociological Theory*. Chicago: Aldine Press. *70–3*

Sedgwick, Peter (1974) R. D. Laing: self, symptom and society. In R. Boyers and R. Orrill (eds) *Laing and Anti-psychiatry*. Harmondsworth: Penguin. *97, 99*

Skinner, B. F. (1972) *Beyond Freedom and Dignity*. London: Jonathan Cape. *56–8, 113*

Spitzer, S. P. and Denzin, N. K. (1968) *The Mental Patient: Studies in the Sociology of Deviance*. New York: McGraw-Hill. *88*

Szasz, T. S. (1960) The myth of mental illness. *Amer. Psychol.* 15: 113–8. *68–9*

Truax, C. B. and Carkhuff, R. R. (1967) *Toward Effective Counseling and Psychotherapy*. Chicago: Aldine. *128*

Watson, Peter (1972) Can racial discrimination affect IQ? In Ken Richardson and David Spears (eds) *Race, Culture and Intelligence*. Harmondsworth: Penguin. *125*

Weisstein, Naomi (1973) Psychology constructs the female. In Phil Brown (ed.) *Radical Psychology*. London: Tavistock Publications. *118*

Wittgenstein, Ludwig (1953) *Philosophical Investigations*. (trans. G. E. M. Anscombe) Oxford: Blackwell. *21*

Young, Jock (1971) *The Drugtakers*. London: Paladin. *50*

Subject Index